REMEMBERING *Lexington* South Carolina

REMEMBERING Lexington South Carolina

Good Stewards in a New Land

Claudette Holliday

THE History PRESS

Published by The History Press
Charleston, SC 29403
www.historypress.net

All images are courtesy of the author.

First published 2008
Second printing 2010
Third printing 2011

Manufactured in the United States

ISBN 978.1.59629.525.4

Library of Congress Cataloging-in-Publication Data

Holliday, Claudette, 1946-
Remembering Lexington, South Carolina : good stewards in a new land / Claudette Holliday.
p. cm.
Includes bibliographical references.
ISBN 978-1-59629-525-4
1. Lexington (S.C.)--History--Anecdotes. 2. Lexington (S.C.)--Biography--Anecdotes. I. Title.
F279.L47H65 2008
975.7'73--dc22
2008022675

This book is dedicated to
Archie Baylis Corley
(1894–1988)

Contents

Contents

Contents

Preface

These stories are about the people, places and events of Lexington County.

My love of history began with my grandfather's stories. His name was Archie Baylis Corley. He was a farmer who descended from Swiss and German farmers, craftsmen, educators, statesmen and settlers in Saxe Gotha and the Dutch Fork more than two hundred years ago. Even though "Mr. Archie" died many years ago, people of our community still fondly remember both him and his stories about Lexington.

Lexington is facing many changes as we enter the twenty-first century. The greatest of these changes is its growth, which sometimes exceeds our ability to cope with its demands. However, we must be ever diligent in keeping our vision fixed upon that which is true and everlasting.

It is my purpose in passing along to you these stories of Lexington to keep the essence of Lexington alive—its character, its charm and its own unique place in South Carolina's history.

Acknowledgements

Jerry and MacLeod Bellune, editor and publisher, respectively, of the *Lexington County Chronicle* and *Dispatch News*, and staff deserve a special thank-you for their encouragement throughout the years.

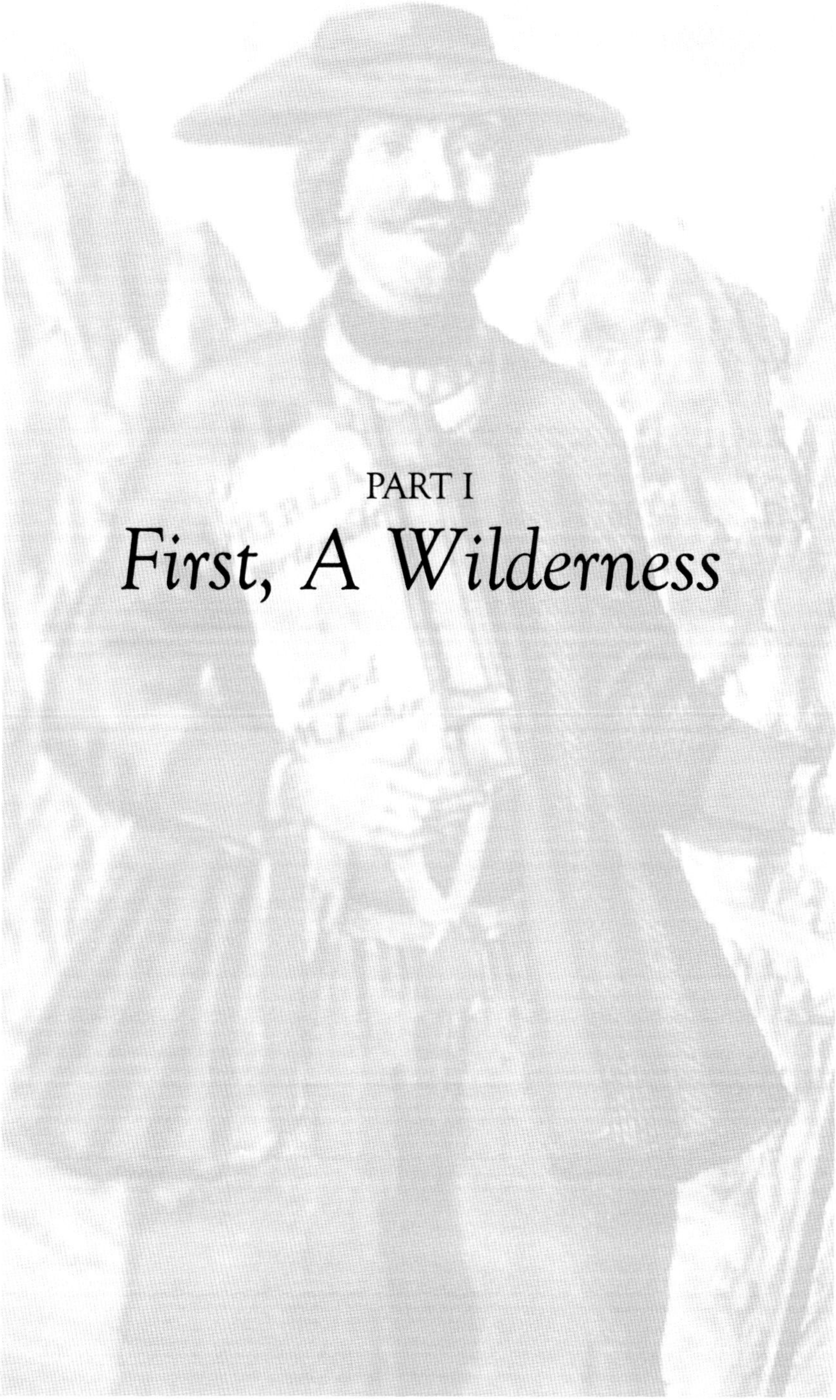

PART I
First, A Wilderness

The Cherokee Path

In 1730, Surveyor General George Hunter mapped out the ancient American Indian trail known as the Cherokee Path. The path extended from Charleston to present-day Tennessee. As a trade route into the interior, it was significant in expanding the frontier and encouraging settlement in South Carolina. In fact, a trade route into the interior was a major consideration in selecting the location of the settlement of Charles Town.

The journey from Charles Town to Keowee (Clemson) took George Hunter and his surveyors fourteen days. Fort Congaree, about midway between Charles Town and Keowee, was located at the junction of two major Native American trade routes and was the result of a treaty between Colonel James Moore and Cherokee Charite Hayge. Settlement began, and the construction of Fort Prince George near Clemson soon followed. Fort Loudon, near current-day Maryville, Tennessee, on the Little Tennessee River, was built in 1752.

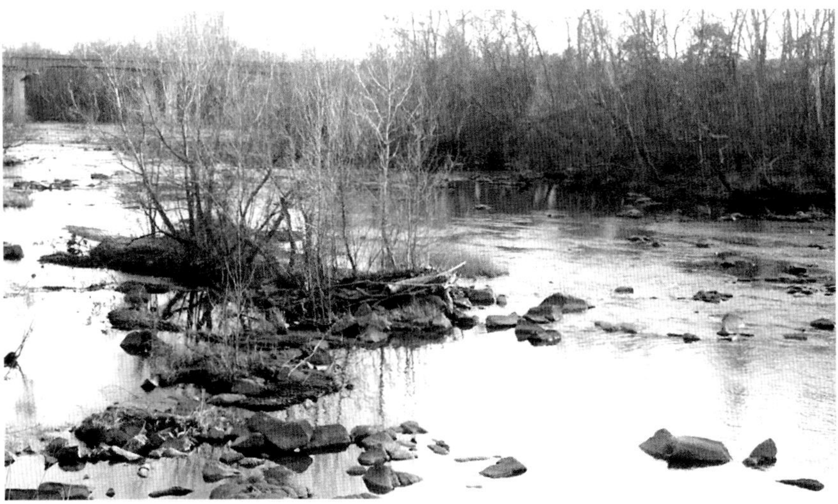

A scenic view of the Congaree River.

In Lexington County, the path enters the county in the south on the route from St. Matthews and runs through the Sandy Run Community, where Herman Geiger had his trading post. Herman Geiger was an early road commissioner who helped expand the footpath into a wagon road system.

From Sandy Run, the path comes to the Congaree Creek at Friday's Ferry and Saxe Gotha. The old roadbed then goes through Cayce to Highway 1, where it follows Leaphart Road to Mineral Springs Road. From there, the path joins Highway 378 and proceeds northwesterly, maintaining its name of Old Cherokee Road. The path turns off Old Cherokee Road onto Beechwood Drive and then again turns onto Highway 378, where it travels into Saluda County to Saluda Old Town.

Once in Saluda County, the path follows the Newberry Road to Ninety Six, Cokesbury, Hodges, Due West, Anderson, Pendleton and on to Fort Loudon.

Many have traveled the path. In addition to the early natives of the Chicora, Cherokee, Edisto, Saluda and Yamassee tribes, De Soto and Don Pardo also discovered the New World along part of our Cherokee Path.

As goods of our own making are shipped to twenty-first-century markets, the old trade route remains an important factor in the consideration of commerce and land development.

Indian Trader Herman Geiger

Today, a granite monument marks the spot where Herman Geiger most likely built his trading post near the Congaree River, twelve miles south of Columbia, just inside the Calhoun County line. In the early days of Lexington's history, Herman Geiger was instrumental in establishing trade in Saxe Gotha Township.

Geiger left for Carolina from the Swiss village of Wydnau in September 1736 with his father, Hans Jacob Gyger, former cantonal governor; his mother, Margareta Feerin; his wife, Elizabeth Habluzel; his children, Catherina and Hans Conrad; and his brothers and sisters, Catherina, Hans Heinrich, Maria Barbara, Hans Jacob and Margareta.

The Geiger family arrived in Charles Town on February 1, 1737. After their arrival, they proceeded to New Windsor and then on to Saxe Gotha, where Herman Geiger established an "Indian" trading post. Upon leaving

New Windsor, John Tobler, author of the *South Carolina Almanac*, considered the departure of the three Geiger men a good riddance, declaring Herman "a useless man…who swore and cursed." Geiger family lands were surveyed in Saxe Gotha above Tom's Creek, next to those of Martin Friday.

One of Geiger's most notable accomplishments in the Carolina backcountry was his role in improving the Cherokee Path into a highway from Charleston to Saxe Gotha during the 1740s, allowing expanded trade.

Early records of the Upper House of the South Carolina Assembly show that Herman Geiger was appointed commissioner of a bridge and causeway at Beaver Creek on June 9, 1747. It was also reported on the same date that Geiger was appointed a commissioner of roads extending from Charles Town into Amelia Township. He also served the colonial governor in his dealings with the Native Americans.

Geiger died in 1751 at age forty-four. It is not known for certain how Herman Geiger met his end, but family legend has it that the Indian trader was clubbed by a local Native American, who was angered by Geiger's attentions toward his squaw. Geiger was then dragged to the creek (probably the Savannah Hunt Creek) and left to die or was drowned. It is accepted knowledge that Geiger's remains are not interred at the memorial site located in the Geiger Cemetery, formerly called Tyler (Taylor) Field Cemetery.

Saxe Gotha

A New Canaan

The year was 1716. Congaree was a lone outpost located about five miles below the mouth of the Saluda River and below the Congaree Creek on the western bank of the Congaree River. It offered little protection for Lowcountry settlements from marauding Native Americans. By 1722, the Congaree garrison was abandoned.

The royal government, still in dire need of a protective buffer for Lowcountry enterprise, ordered the Township Act of 1733 to place settlers across the Native American trading path and deter Lowcountry Indian raids. In total, there were eleven townships planned, with twenty thousand acres of land in each.

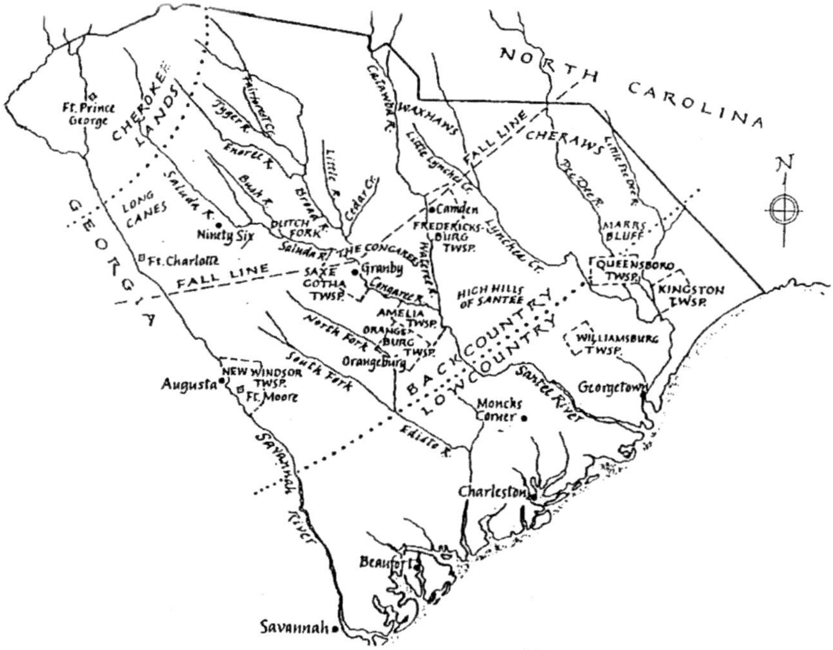

A map of early settlements in South Carolina.

They were to be situated along the Altamaha, Savannah, Pee Dee, Waccamaw, Wateree, Black, Santee, Congaree and Edisto Rivers. The Altamaha eventually became part of Georgia.

Some of the first to arrive along the frontier were Indian traders. Thomas Brown, with his brother Patrick of Northern Ireland, was the first to establish trade with the Catawbas, building a store at Congaree in 1733. In 1735, Swiss bounty settlers began arriving. Among these settlers were Martin Friday, John Ulric Muller, Jacob Gallman, John Matthias, Jacob Spuhl and John Ulirc Bachman.

The Cherokee Path was soon widened into a wagon road above Amelia Township to accommodate trade. River navigation was also begun, further benefiting Saxe Gotha.

Jacob Gallman described Saxe Gotha in a letter:

> *After spending three weeks in Charlestown we were taken to Congaree. Each person was given axes and a hoe and one half acre for a home and garden in the town. After that we were given thirty acres of land for each person, free for ten years and provisions for one year…there is a river near our place, it*

runs down to Charlestown. It is a river full of ships and many good fish. There are many deer here and traders ride here with twenty or thirty horses with brandy, shot, muskets, plantation utensils, straps and deer hides…there would be room for many more people. It is good country, almost compared with Canaan or an earthly paradise.

Christian Theus

Teacher and Minister

The community of Sandy Run is in the horse's neck in southern Lexington County near Calhoun County. Sandy Run Lutheran Church has its place in early Saxe Gotha history. Its congregation dates back to Swiss/German settlement and the Reverend Christian Theus, who is buried in its peaceful cemetery. It bore the name of Salem when it was incorporated into the Corpus Evangelicum of 1787.

The congregation probably began sometime prior to 1751. It had its share of misfortune and disease, and the church was moved and rebuilt several times.

In 1770, the church moved farther inland along the Sandy Run Creek to avoid floods on the fever-prone Congaree River. A third move came in 1800, when Lutherans, Baptists and Methodists worshipped together at the old meetinghouse. In 1823, a fourth church was built; it burned in 1917. A fifth, the current church, was completed in 1919.

Sandy Run Lutheran Church's first ministers saw the congregation through many of its early trials of faith. They were Theus; Lewis Hockheiner; the Reverends Walleran, Dasher, Franklow and Yost Metz; and William Berly—all builders of Lexington's strong Lutheran foundation.

Theus's grave was moved in 1932 from the site of the Reformed Lutheran Church of Congarees, which was located seven miles northwest of old Saxe Gotha Township, where he served for over fifty years as minister and teacher to immigrant settlers like himself.

Theus came to Carolina with his parents and brothers, Jeremiah and Simeon, from Gaubunden, Switzerland. He was ordained by the Reverend English Presbyterian Ministries and began his ministry in 1739. In 1748, he was married by the Reverend Gessendanner to "N.N.," as noted in Gessendanner's journal. Theus, too, kept a journal, which has been located in a library in the state of Utah.

Reverend Theus did his part in bringing freedom of worship to the backcountry. He worked in establishing St. John's Pomaria, Zion, St. Jacob's Wateree and other congregations. He is most remembered for his encounter with the infamous Weberites along the Saluda River, an encounter that ended in the trial and hanging of Jacob Weber and the expulsion of Weberite followers from Saxe Gotha. Christian Theus was the last of the old Reformed ministers of the county. When Theus died, the Reformed faith in Lexington ceased.

The Weberite Heresy

It was along the Saluda River at Younginer's Ferry where the infamous Weberite incident occurred. Not too many years ago, you could look eastward down the Saluda River at the Lake Murray Dam and see the remains of old Younginer's Ferry.

Among the devout Reformed congregation of Switzers' Neck and Saluda Fork was a sect called the Weberites. The sect was founded by Peter Schmidt and spread into North Carolina, Maryland and Virginia sometime around 1760. Jacob Weber and his family lived across the Saluda River from the site of the old Zion Church. Several families of the community joined with Schmidt and Weber. The Reverend Dr. Muhlenberg gives us an account of the incident from his journal.

> *The people of the backcountry, in general, grew up without schools and instruction. Occasionally a self-taught Minister may labor for a while amongst them, yet it continues only a short time. The people are wild and continue to grow wilder, for what does it profit them to hear a sermon every four, six, or twelve weeks, if in early youth the foundation of Divine Truth had not been laid? The Weberite sect had so far obtained the supremacy that several families united with it for fear of their lives; numbers of both sexes went about uncovered and naked, and practiced the most abominable wantonness. One of them pretended to be God the Father, another the Son,*

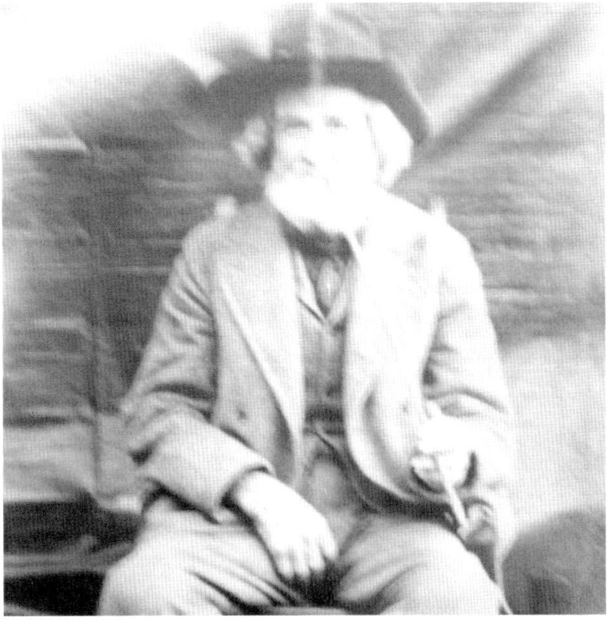

David Smithpeter, great-grandson of Johnannes George Smithpeter of Switzers' Neck.

and a third, the Holy Spirit. The pretended Father, having quarreled with the Son, repudiated the pretended Son, chained him in the forest, declared him to be Satan, and finally gathered his gang who beat and trampled on the poor man until he died; he is reported also to have killed the pretended Holy Ghost in bed. A report of these circumstances having reached the authorities in Charleston, the Militia was ordered to arrest the pretended deity, where upon he was tried, condemned, and executed upon the gallows.

The *South Carolina Gazette* reported the incident on April 18, 1761:

On the 5th Ult. some unhappy wretches, in a fit of religious delusions and enthusiasm, had in a most barbarous manner, murdered one Michael Hans and Captain John George Smith Peter on the 23rd and 24th of February last at Congarees, were brought down from thence and committed to jail. Their delusion was so great that they acknowledged the murders, and for some days attempted to justify themselves. But at March session they were too well convinced of their error, when seven of them were indicted and tried and four convicted viz. Jacob Weber, John Geiger, Jacob Bourghart, and Hannah Weber who all received the sentence of death of the 31st Ult. And on the 17th instant, Jacob Weber was hanged pursuant to his sentence, behaving in a very becoming manner, and dying a true penitent; the other three were reproved 'till May.

On May 18, 1761, the *South Carolina Gazette* reported:

At a court of common plea held this week, before the honorable William Simpson, Esq., Chief Justice, were John Geiger, Jacob Bourghart, and Hannah Weber (who, with Jacob Weber, executed on the 17th Ult. were convicted of murder at March sessions, and received the sentence of death the 31st of the same month) were admitted to bail, to appear upon recognizance from session to session, 'til his Majesty's pleasure touching the sentence passed upon them shall be known.

In the *Southern Christian Advocate*, on Thursday, May 14, 1931, Claude E. Leitner wrote:

It will be recalled that prior to 1775 the Episcopal Church was the established church in South Carolina, and dissenters had a hard time of it because of that fact. The Saxe Gotha church will fairly illustrate this. In Saxe Gotha (Lexington) on the banks of the Saluda dwelt a number of pious German people who formed a congregation which was broken up in disgrace by a so-called "trial of Weberite heretics." It was alleged that their religious leaders, Weber, Schmidt, and Repsimann, had misappropriated the title Father, Son, and Holy Ghost, and had actually done to death the person representing the Devil. We smile at such nonsense, but they actually hanged Weber for it. When they had taken him to Charleston, and as we would say today "railroaded" him through the Court. Jacob Weber, imprisoned and ironed, signed a confession worth going to Charleston to see. There is not a German expression in it, and Weber was as German as sauerkraut. Even the nouns and principle words are not capitalized. The rector of a certain church in Charleston certainly knew how to write a good confession, even if he was ignorant of German and Germans. But Schmidt and Repsimann, and certain others of these persecuted families moved over the Broad River and settled in the Cedar Creek neighborhood where Schmidt was Smith and Repsimann was Turnipseed, and for four or five generations their descendants have given the lie to the Weberite Heresy. Unordained, the Repsimanns, et. al., undertook to meet the needs of their day. But the numerous Nipper, Leitner, Kilgo, and Turnipseed preachers which have literally covered South Carolina and Florida are and have been of the same grade of heretic.

The following is an excerpt from Jacob Weber's letter, dated April 16, 1761, that he wrote to his children before he was executed, desiring to "transmit to my beloved children a sketch of my mournful life." He stated:

> *I, Jacob Weber, was born in Switzerland, in Canton Zurich, in the County of Knomauer, in the parish of Stifferschwill, and was raised and educated in the Reformed Church. In the fourteenth year of my life I journeyed with my brother to South Carolina, leaving my parents; and soon after my arrival lost my brother in death. Thus, I was forsaken of man, and without father or mother.*
>
> *And now my children, beloved in the Lord, I must leave this world, and perhaps behold your face no more in this life. I command you, therefore, to the protection and mercy of God! Pray without ceasing, learn and read, injure no one willingly and willfully while you live; labor industriously and faithfully according to your ability. May God preserve all persons from so great a fall, and trample Satan under foot, for Christ sake, Amen.*

Weber's wife, Hannah, was pardoned, and "all traces of this abominable heresy disappeared, and no descendants of Weber or Schmidt were to be found in the Saluda Fork."

Lexington County equity records give a hint as to those involved in the Weberite Heresy. John Conrad Geiger was married to Barbara, whose estate papers provided the following:

> *Both Murph and Geiger families were Swiss, the Geigers being from the Rheinthal, where immigrant Hans Jacob Geiger was once been Cantonal Governor. This family is related to the Geiger family associated with the Salzbuergers of Georgia, which descends from Abraham Geiger, who was banished from South Carolina for his part in the Weberite Heresy, in which he was one of the twelve Apostles who gathered around Weber when he claimed to be God the Father.*

Log Cabins on the Frontier

The Laurance Corley log cabin is one of the oldest standing structures in Lexington County and represents the frontier era of old Orangeburg District. It has been carbon dated at around 1771. Its location was once part of a 620-acre tract between the Fourteen and Twelve Mile Creeks on the waters of the Saluda. The land was granted to Laurance Corley in 1804. Barbara Housar appears to have first been granted the lands in 1747.

The Corley cabin has been moved twice. Its first location was on the Twelve Mile Creek. It was later moved to a location near Heritage Hills at the end of Corley Street. Laurance Corley's first wife, Christina, is buried near the site. It is possible that the cabin was part of a larger homestead and was perhaps used as a kitchen or a schoolroom. Cooking was done apart from the main house, and baking was done in an outdoor bake oven. A favorite dish of the settlers was rice pudding served with sangaree, which was placed in a scooped-out hollow in the center of the pudding.

Settlers of early Orangeburg District were rugged frontiersmen whose lifestyles were simple and basic. They were small farmers, craftsmen and merchants known for their thriftiness, loyalty and honesty. Many in South Carolina's backcountry sought refuge from the tyrannical religious principalities of southern Germany and Switzerland.

In the years following the American Revolution, the frontier grew into a center of trade. An independent, frontier-style strength of character is reflected in the descendants of the early settlers' attitudes toward success. Cotton was introduced to the area between 1820 and 1830, and with it came the opportunity of great wealth. Many farmers believed the coming of cotton meant the beginning of society's downfall, and cotton's easy riches symbolized gluttony and greed.

After Laurance Corley's death in 1820, additions were made to the cabin. During this period, between 1818 and 1820, the county seat was moved from Granby to Lexington. The cabin was abandoned in 1900, and it was not until 1930 that Tom and Reba Corley rented the cabin to a Mr. and Mrs. Gates and the cabin was remodeled. Many families lived in the cabin in the years that followed.

Finally, in 1975, the log cabin was moved to the Lexington County Museum, where it remains today.

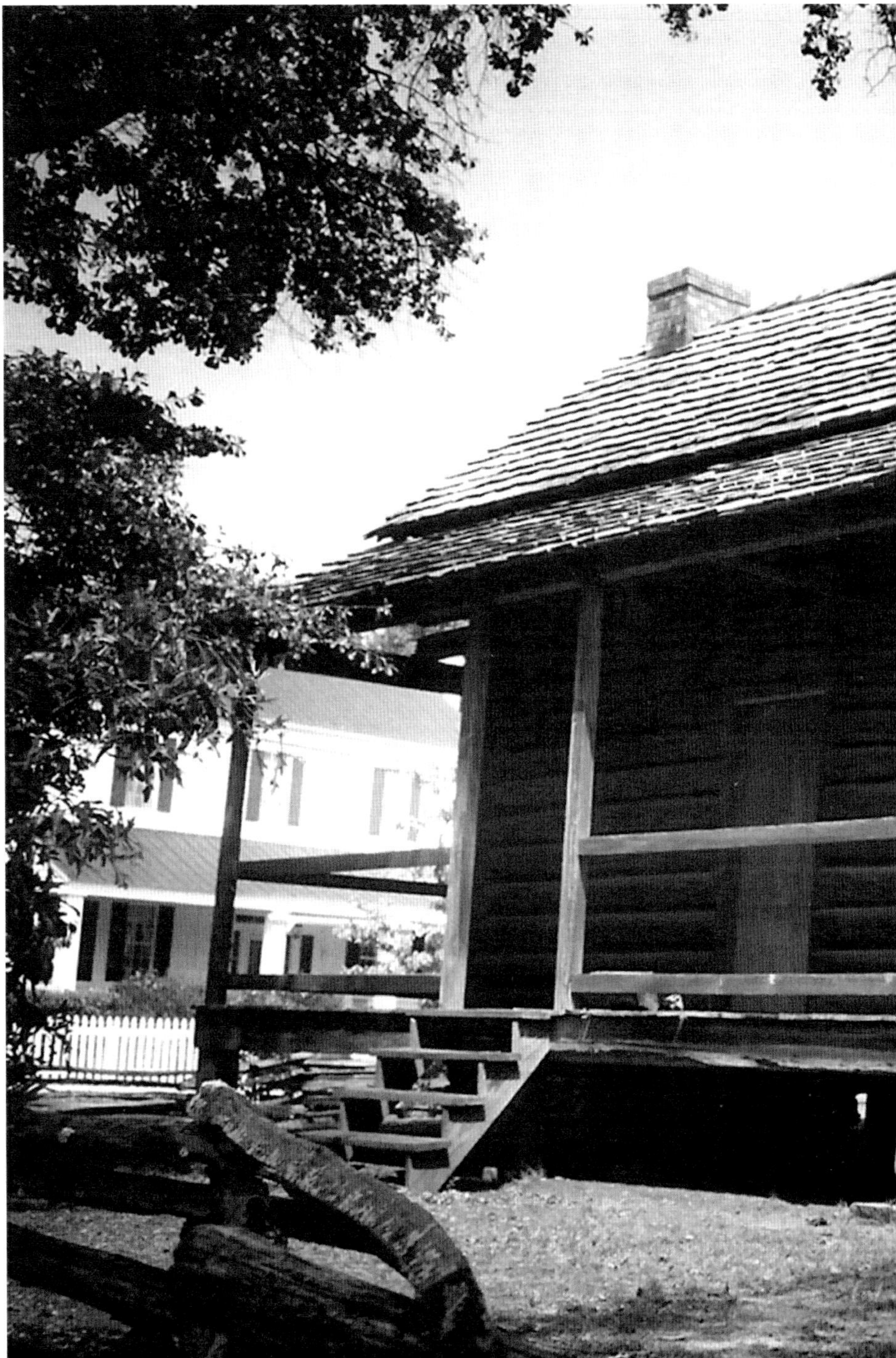

Laurance Corley's log house. Lexington was built on the Corley plantation.

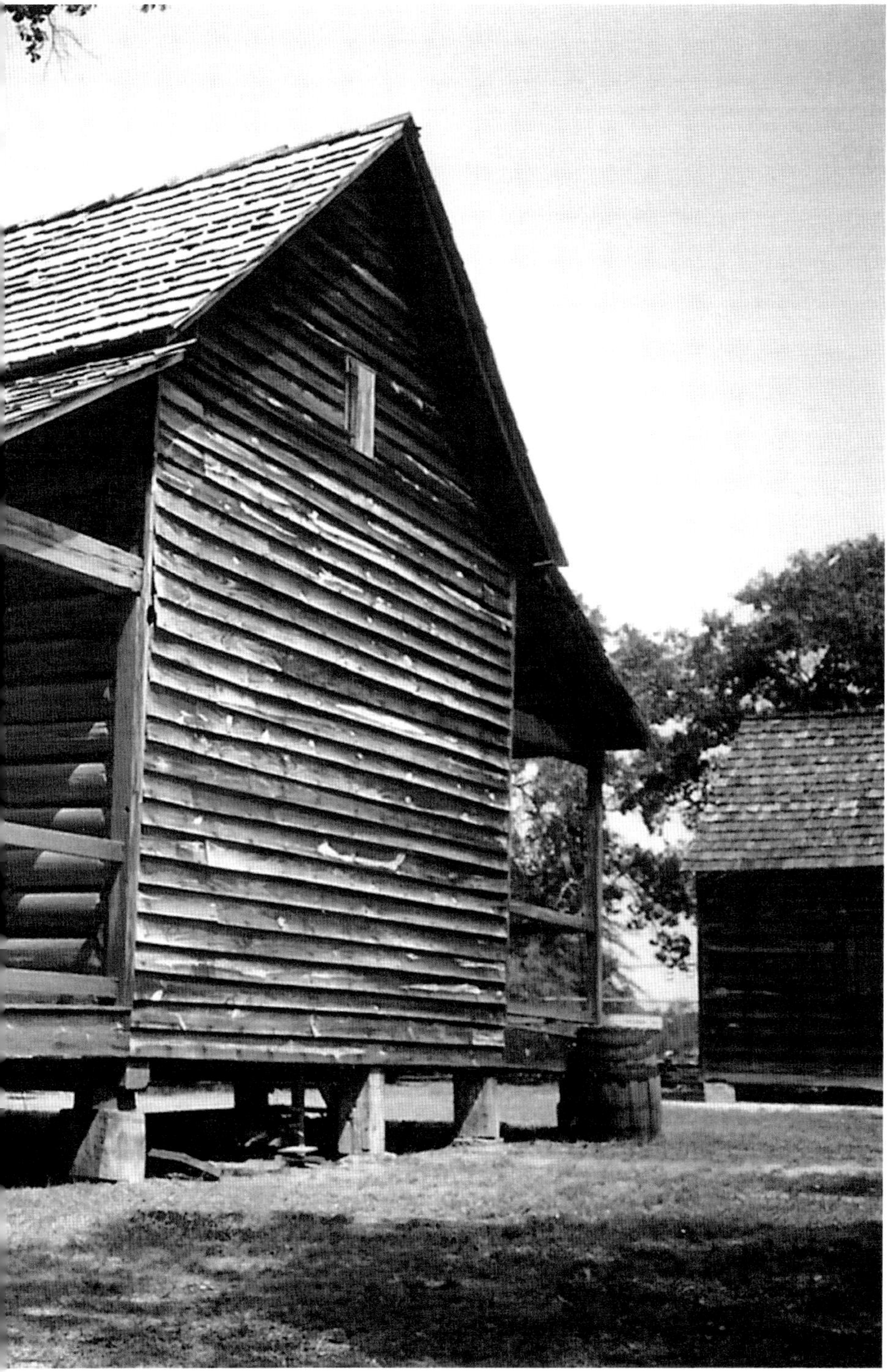

Trouble in Saxe Gotha

In the spring of 1746, the settlers of Saxe Gotha got a good taste of English intentions for settlements of the backcountry—they were to be a buffer for the Lowcountry against Native Americans from the West and North.

Immigrants had left homes and villages in Switzerland only to be confronted by an old enemy—the French and their American Indian allies—in their new homes in the Carolina backcountry. France, Spain and Prussia were engaged in the War of Succession with England, Holland and Austria in the years following the death of Austria's Charles X in 1740. This war's tentacles followed European quests for dominance and territorial possession to the New World. Swiss settlers found themselves caught up in this feud as they heard stories of brutality against their Protestant kinsmen left behind in Basel at the hands of Catholic Prince-Bishop Jacob Sigmund von Reinach, an ally of their French enemy. While on the expanding frontier, the French at Mobile were aligning themselves with Western and Northern American Indian tribes to challenge the British along the East Coast.

In 1725, all was peaceful along the Congaree River. Fort Congaree had been abandoned, and trade with local Native Americans was flourishing. By 1746, this peace was being eroded by French influence on the western frontier. After nearly a year of mounting fears, the sudden appearance of a marauding band of Chickasaws brought the settlers face to face with allies of their old French enemy. Although the band plundered the settlers' homes and destroyed many of their belongings, the threat of attack was exaggerated. Nonetheless, fear prompted the settlement to petition the assembly at Charles Town for protection. The council journals record these fears:

> *They are in a dangerous situation and leading a perilous life, as the Township was more exposed to the Incursions of the Indians than perhaps any other Frontier place which lay open and upon the adjoining Paths from the North and West, and that their homes being in a row along the River Side, might easily be surrounded, and they singly destroyed by any small Party without their being able to give Notice to the Neighbors, and that in case an alarm was made, they had no fixed place where to meet, and no where to secure their wives and children.*

By 1748, there were 200 inhabitants in Saxe Gotha. In 1749, another 250 Palatine settlers arrived in Saxe Gotha with John Jacob Reimensperger. Many

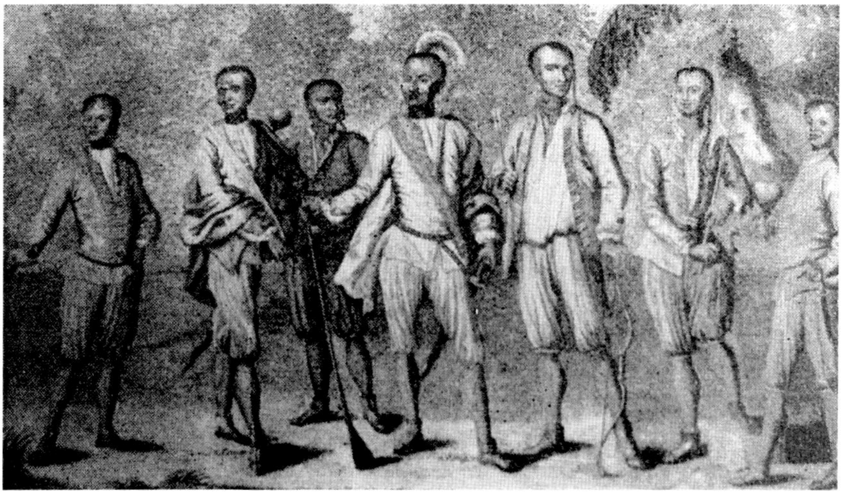

This delegation of Cherokee chiefs went to London in 1730 to see King George II.

of these Germans settled above Saxe Gotha in the Dutch Fork between the Saluda and Broad Rivers. Saxe Gotha Township was located between Sandy Run on the southern end of the Congaree River and Twelve Mile Creek on the northern end of the Saluda River.

The town of Saxe Gotha was laid out near the old garrison, with its front street paralleling the river for nearly a mile. Fort Fairchild was located on the northern boundary of the township.

The economic life of Saxe Gotha was largely dependent upon Native American trade. In 1747, Thomas Brown died. His trade was soon taken up by Herman Geiger and lasted until Geiger died in 1751. Robert Steill, a member of a Charleston firm, also settled on the Congaree to trade with the Catawbas after Brown's death.

Another important trader in Saxe Gotha was George Haig. Native Americans killed Haig in 1748. With the loss of these key men, trade shifted northwesterly toward Ninety Six, where one of Geiger's clients, Robert Goudy, continued his Indian trade. With Haig's murder, the assembly provided for a second Fort Congaree near Christian Theus's church, St. John's, and two troops of rangers to patrol the frontier during these dangerous times. The garrison was maintained for several years.

The commander at Fort Moore said of the white hunters' skills at the Saluda and Congaree: "For they are in general very expert woodsmen, but might exceed their orders as they are little more than White Indians." The chief route to the Cherokees began at Fort Moore in the earlier part of the 1700s,

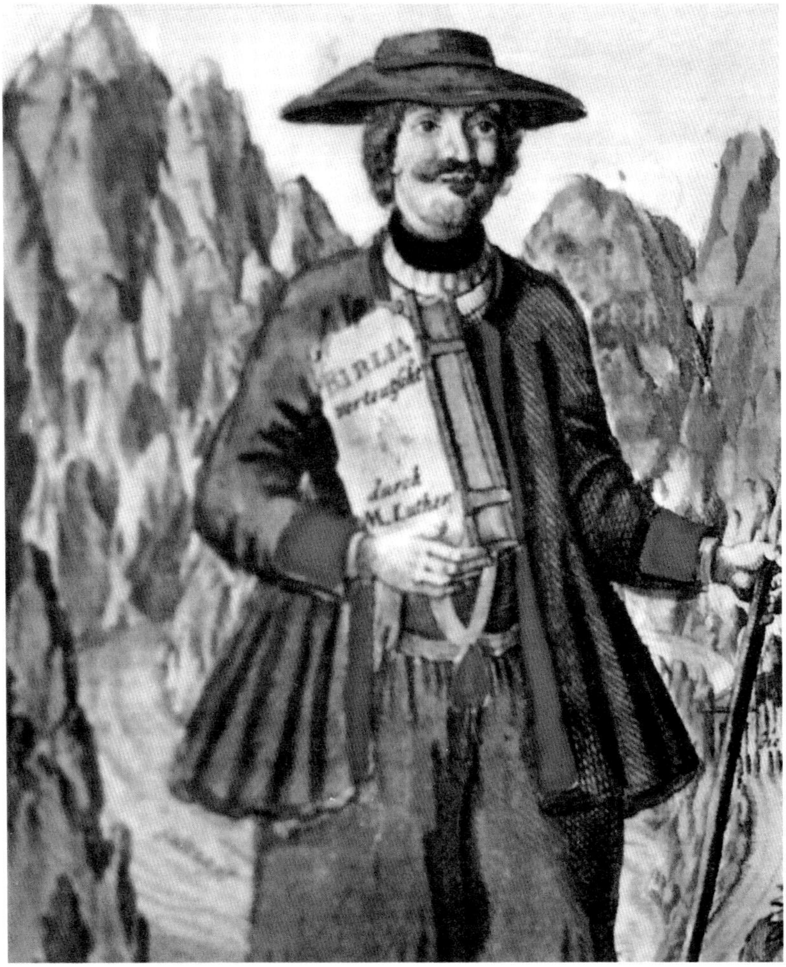

Swiss immigrants came to Saxe Gotha Township in 1734 to defend the Carolina frontier.

but moved toward the Congaree and Santee settlements with the opening of wagon roads and river navigation.

The township of Saxe Gotha was a defensive success. Passage from the mountains to the coastal plain was being defended by a population of sturdy frontiersmen and their families.

Savanno Indians Attack

Much of what is now Lexington County was inhabited by Savanno Indians by 1764, although the Congaree and Saluda were close neighbors of Saxe Gotha. The Savannos were part of the Shawnee, whose homeland was the Cumberland River and whose relatives could be found in Lancaster, Pennsylvania. The Savanno were allies of the Iroquois, the Delaware and the French.

The Savannos ravaged the Carolina backcountry settlers into the 1750s. In May 1751, a mixed band of Notowegas attacked the home of retired Indian trader Isaac Cloud, who lived along Cloud's Creek in northwestern Lexington County. Mary Cloud, Isaac's wife, narrowly escaped the ordeal. Although mortally wounded, she made her way to the home of Martin Friday at Saxe Gotha and gave the following account of the incident:

> *That on the fourth instant two Indians came to my House about Halfway between the Congarees and Savannah Town. The Indians were Savannas. They came there about dark, and sate down very civilly; and my Husband being able to talk their Tongue they talked a great while together, and I gave them supper. And they asked my Husband for Pipes and Tobacco, and he gave it them. And we sate up until midnight, and then we all went to sleep; and they lay down too and pulled off their mogassens and boots. One of them broke his pipe, and he came to the bed of my Husband, who handed him his pipe out of his Mouth, and laid down again; and we all dropt into sleep; and when the cocks began to crow they came, as I suppose, to the Bed and shot my Husband through the Head. And a young man lying upon the floor was Shot in the same minute. And the Indians, I suppose, thinking the Bullet had gone through my Husband's Head and my own too, struck me with a Tomahawk under my right Arm; and afterwards they struck me two Cuts upon the left Knee. I lying still they supposed I was dead, and one of them went and killed both my Children; and then they came and took the blankets from us and plundered the House of all that was valuable and went off. And in that bad Condition I have lain amongst my Dead two Days. And by the help of Providence one of my Horses came to the House; and so I came to Martin Friday's House.*

Mary Cloud died of her wounds, and the colonial government arranged to pay the doctor who cared for her, her nurse and her funeral charges. The Savannos continued their attacks on the settlers until the end of the Revolutionary War.

The Cherokee Wars and Removal to the West

Settlements of the Carolina backcountry experienced the full horrors of warfare during the uprisings of the 1760s. The Cherokee, too, were finally warring with their European neighbors. John Pearson reported the following Native American activities to Governor Bull:

> *They have burnt and destroyed all up the Bush River, where there are some people gathered to stand in their own defense; all up the Saludy Little River, Rabourne's Creek, Long Canes and Steven's Creeks are all destroyed. I am informed they have killed twenty-seven persons on Rabourne's Creek, and out of 200 persons that were settled on Long Canes Creek and Steven's Creek not above forty or fifty are to be found, so that the case is very desperate, and all the people that move down hardly stop at the Congarees.*

The Long Canes incident that occurred on February 1, 1760, is one of the best reported of these Native American attacks. John C. Calhoun's grandmother was one of the backcountry settlers killed at Long Canes as she fled her home for the safety of Augusta. It was reported in the *South Carolina Gazette* that about one hundred mounted American Indian raiders attacked and killed about fifty white men, women and children, destroyed thirteen loaded wagons and carts and enslaved survivors.

An incident at Fort Prince George set off war with the Middle Settlement Cherokees. The commanding officer of the fort, Lieutenant Cotymore, was killed in an ambush. In retaliation, an entire band of Cherokee warriors being held at Fort Prince George was brutally slain by the soldiers. As a result, hostilities quickly spread more than one hundred miles in all directions, and settlers were forced to seek refuge in the Lowcountry. Many who escaped into the woods died of starvation.

Captain James Francis of the Ninety Six District reported to the governor:

> *We by leave to acquaint your excellency, that we had the pleasure during the engagement to see several of your enemy drop; and we now have the pleasure,*

> *Sir, to fatten our dogs with their carcasses, and to display their scalps, neatly ornamented, on the top of our bastions.*

The Cherokee War ended on November 19, 1761. The war cost many innocent lives and impoverished both white and Native American South Carolinians. By 1796, most of the Lower Cherokees had moved to Alabama along the Coosa River. In March 1816, a treaty was signed with the Cherokees ceding the last Cherokee lands in South Carolina to the state for $5,000. The Savannos had crossed the Mississippi into Ohio, Missouri and Indiana and eventually submitted to removal in 1869, joining the Cherokee Nation of Indian Territory, Oklahoma.

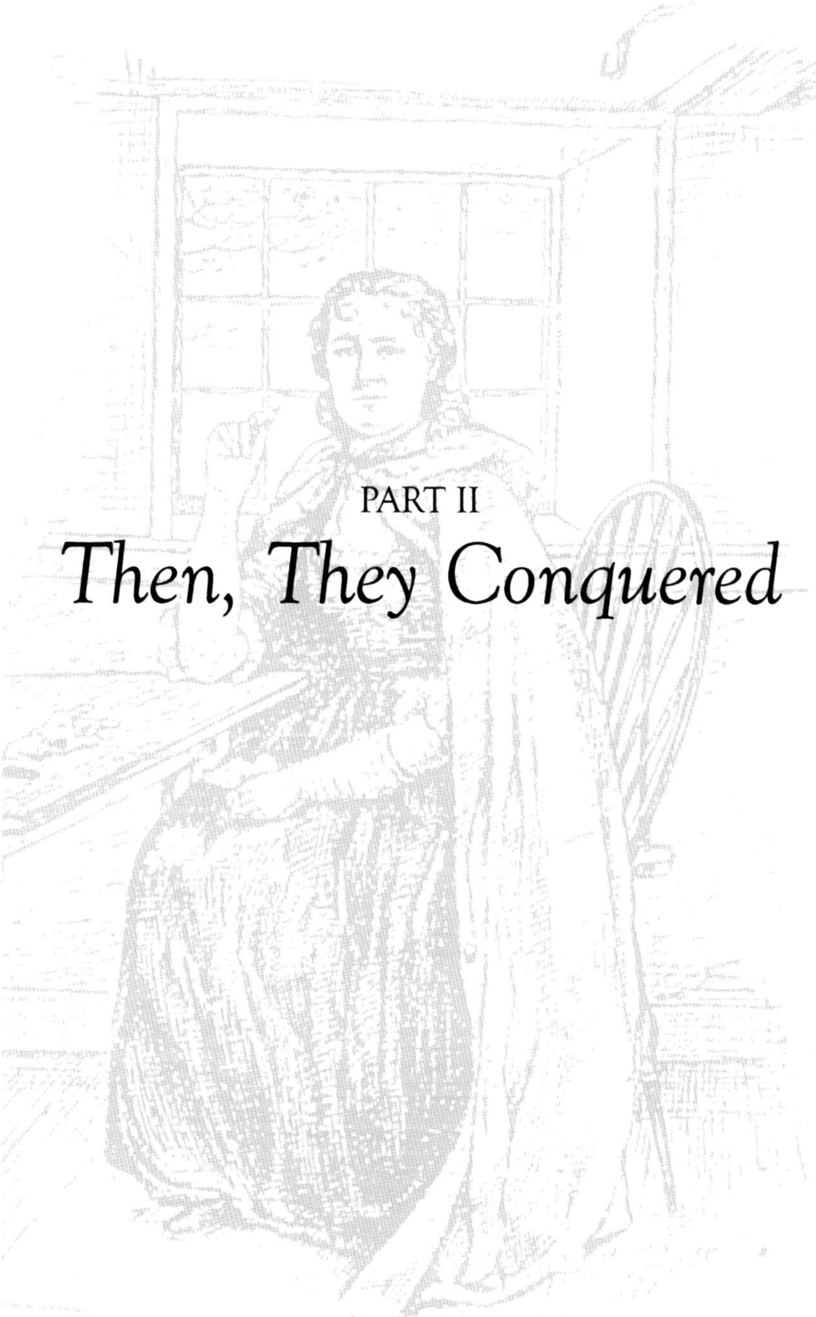

PART II
Then, They Conquered

Fort Granby

In the years following the American Revolution, Benson J. Lossing revisited important military sites throughout the fledgling country. The following account is taken from his *Pictorial Field-Book of the American Revolution*, volume two, as told to Lossing by an aging and invalid James Cayce.

The Cayce house was the Fort Granby of the American Revolution. It was located near the old State Road to Charleston and nearly a mile from Friday's river crossing. The Cayce house at the time of Lossing's visit was located near the site of the old village, now desolate, with only a few unoccupied dwellings remaining.

The Cayce home was originally built by Camden merchants to store cotton and other goods before they were shipped down the river to the coast. During the Revolution, the home was fortified with a ditch and parapet. A garrison of 290 Loyalists and 90 Hessians led by the inexperienced Colonel Maxwell of Maryland's Eastern Shore occupied the fort.

On May 15, 1781, American forces led by Light Horse Harry Lee freed Fort Granby from British occupation in a bloodless encounter. It was on this same day that General Sumter took Orangeburg and General Rawdon was retreating toward Charleston. The little American army encamped at Fort Granby had cause for celebration. The Cayce house proudly bears scars left by Patriot bullets, cannon fire and British axes.

Lossing's footnote reveals something about the local families and their loyalties:

> *Mr. Friday (Gabriel), James Cayce's father-in-law, and his brother were the only Whigs of that name in the state, and often suffered insults from their Tory kinsmen. Mr. Friday owned mills at Granby and also a ferry called by his name. When the British fortified that post the garrison supplied themselves with flour from his establishment. He gave the British the credit of dealing honorably; paying him liberally for everything they took from him—flour, poultry, cattle, etc. On one occasion, when called to the fort to receive his pay, Colonel Maxwell said to him, "Mr. Friday, I hope you are as clever a fellow as those of your name who are with us." "No,"*

shouted his Tory uncle, "he's a damned Rebel, and I'll split him down!" while at the same time rushing forward to execute his brutal purpose.

After the battle at Eutaw Springs, Colonel Maxwell, passing through Granby, stopped one night at Mr. Friday's. The Colonel remarked, "Mr. Friday, you are a friend of your country. Remain so. We have not yet conquered it, and never will. Your name will be honored, while those of your countrymen who are with us will be despised." Captain Gabriel Friday equipped and led a company of men for General Sumter with his own funds.

Granby Village

In 1760, Granby Village, which was named for the Earl of Granby, who was the commander in chief of the British army, was one of the most important trading centers east of the Mississippi River.

Saxe Gotha Township, the original settlement at the Congarees, had fallen into decline. The settlers had chosen to claim their grants on farmlands farther up the river valley instead of in the flood-prone, 919-acre township along the river. Job Marion, brother of Francis Marion, claimed these lands in 1770. His home, however, was in St. John's Parish above Charleston.

In the early 1800s, Granby was much larger than Columbia, located on the eastern side of the Congaree on a high plain. In March 1785, Granby had become the county seat of Lexington. There were large stores, warehouses, hotels and a post office. Arthur Fort was senator of the district between 1782 and 1784. Richard Hampton followed him in office until 1791.

As Columbia grew, Granby declined for many of the same reasons that Saxe Gotha declined. Land around the river had been cleared for farming, making it even more prone to flooding. Edwin Scott reflected on Granby in *Random Recollections of a Long Life*:

> *The town being at the head of navigation on the Congaree with a ferry on the road leading to the up country, and broad fertile river swamp lands extending many miles below, was a place of considerable business, and some of its merchants made fortunes and lived in good style. Their families were well educated and formed a circle of refined society.*

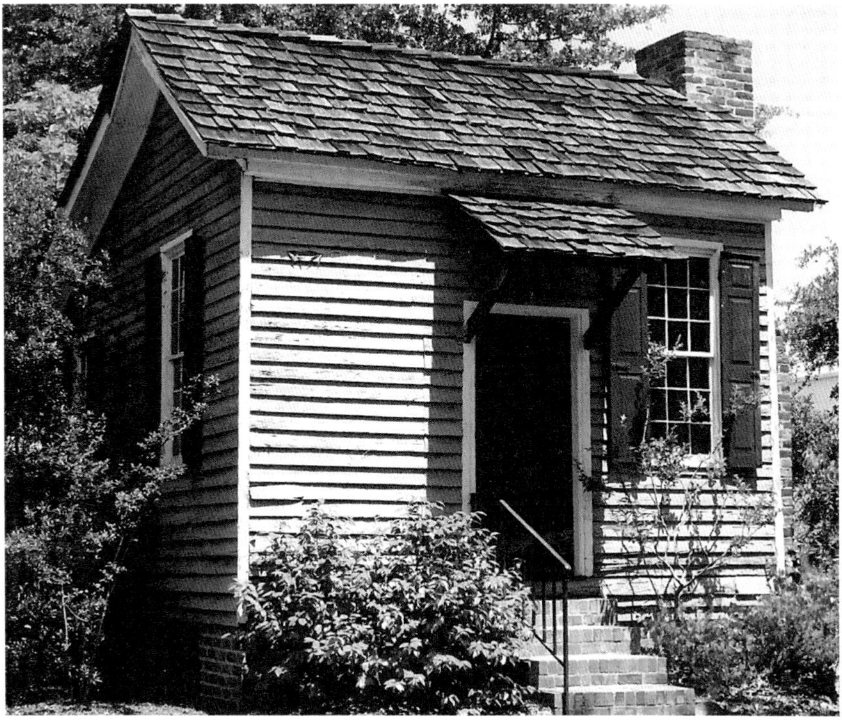

This is perhaps the oldest structure in Lexington County. It once served as a law office in Granby, a post office and doctor's office in Lexington and is now part of the Lexington County Museum.

Among the families were the Cayces, Arthurs, Fridays, Seibles, Hanes and others. By 1822, Granby was a deserted village and the county seat was moved to Lexington Courthouse on the Twelve Mile Creek.

Many of the buildings in Granby were moved. Some were taken to the Saluda factory, but the elegant courthouse was moved to 1400 Lady Street, in Columbia, where it served as the Presbyterians' first church for over forty years.

In 1853, the Granby courthouse was moved again—across the street—where it served as a theological school. J.R. Niernsie bought the house to live in while he oversaw the construction of the statehouse. The courthouse was later owned by a Captain Waites and finally was bought by John Kinard. Today, nothing remains of Granby's renowned courthouse.

Godfrey Dreher and the Tories

Zion's church book records an amazing tale about how Godfrey Dreher outsmarted the Tories. Unquestionably, Godfrey Dreher commanded respect and admiration among his neighbors. He watched over his flock, which numbered as many as six hundred at one point in Zion's history. As their pastor and protector, Godfrey Dreher was seemingly supernatural.

At the celebration of Zion's centennial in August 1892, the Reverend E.L. Lybrand delivered the following account of Reverend Dreher's abilities.

Godfrey Dreher lived near Twelve Mile Creek mill (Loricks's and later Corley's). It is recorded that he was the grantor of this land to Zion Church. His large, two-story home served as a fort during the American Revolution and provided the community of Switzers' Neck protection from the Tories who roamed these parts, harassing and murdering Patriots.

On one occasion, as many as twelve or fifteen Tories came galloping up to Mr. Dreher's, expecting to butcher the residents. Mr. Dreher used cunning strategy and courage to defeat them. He had provided for himself a drum and a violin and had chains in the house. All of these things were upstairs, and the residents were taught, on the approach of the enemy, to make a loud noise as though there were many people inside.

Old Mr. Dreher stationed himself below, and as the band of Tories rode up, he gave loud orders to those above. They promptly began drumming, fiddling and throwing the chains about. The lead Tory entered the doorway. As he did, Dreher shot him down and called for the crowd from above to come down quickly. The Tories were so frightened by the noise that they fled in great confusion, leaving most of their horses for Dreher.

In 1788, the legislature incorporated fifteen "Dutch" churches. Zion was one of these. It served as both a Lutheran and Reformed church for many years. There is substantial evidence that Zion was actually 150 years old in 1892. Although the original grants have been lost, evidence suggests that Zion was an active church as early as 1740.

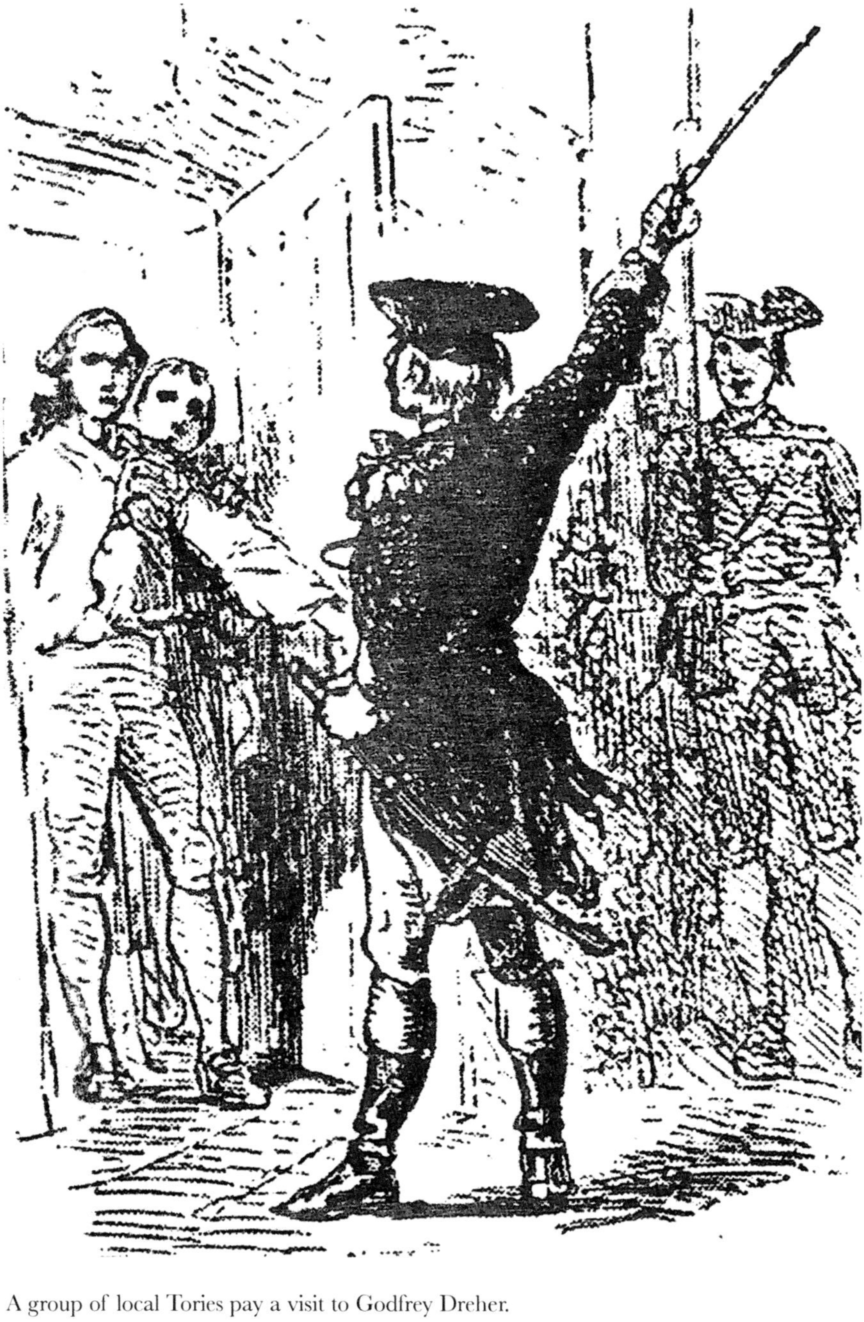

A group of local Tories pay a visit to Godfrey Dreher.

Laurance Corley

American Patriot

Laurance Corley lived in Lexington two hundred years ago. How he lived and who he was can be glimpsed in the things he left behind. One of these is the Corley log cabin on the grounds of the Lexington County Museum.

On Sunday, June 29, 1997, Laurance Corley's descendants dedicated a marker. An accurate count has not been tabulated reflecting just how many descendants Laurance Corley does have, but suffice it to say, as the local saying does, "If you throw a rock in Lexington you're going to hit at least two Corleys." The descendants of John, Daniel, Elizabeth and William spoke up to be counted, but there were others, too.

Laurance Corley was the father of sixteen children: John, Daniel, Jacob, Elizabeth, Barbara, Catherine, Emanuel and Ephraim by his first wife, Christina; and Nancy, Sally, William, Thomas, Mary Ann, Elijah, Jemima and Rebecca by his second wife, Barbara Derrick Drafts "Granny" Corley.

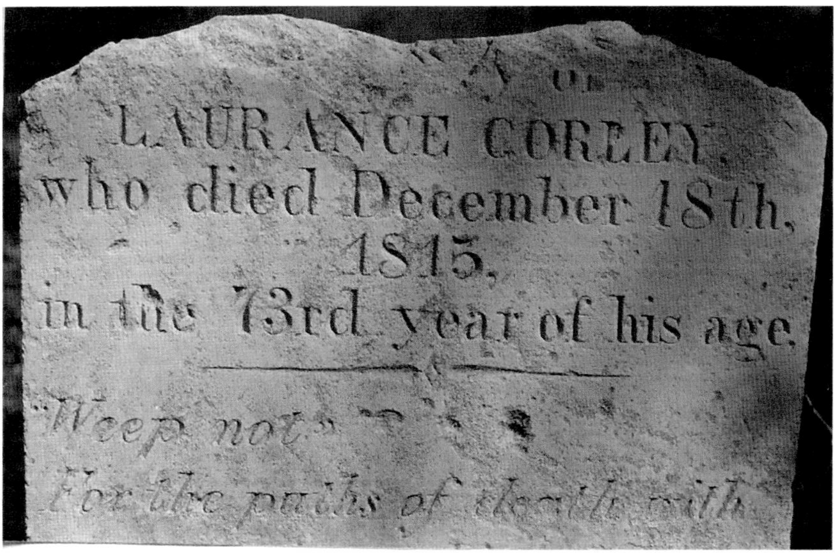

Laurance Corley's grave marker, located in the town of Lexington.

At the dedication there were speeches, cheers and the sounds of patriotic music. This is something else Laurance Corley left behind—sociable people who celebrate life and the bounty of a fruitful nation, feasting at the table of liberty and freedom.

Congressman Floyd Spence addressed Corley's descendants on the importance of family in the building of a country. The congressman, too, is part of Corley's family.

Laurance Corley and many of his neighbors, under the leadership of Captain Gabriel Friday, defeated the British in the Lexington District during the American Revolution. They are remembered.

Emily Geiger's Ride

Emily Geiger was a young woman of about sixteen or eighteen years when she volunteered to serve the cause of American independence with her famous ride through Lexington District and enemy lines.

At the time, Emily was living at her family's home near the junction of the Broad and Enoree Rivers. She cared for her invalid father, Hans. The Geigers were descendants of immigrant Hans Conrad von Geiger, secretary to the king of Wurttemberg, and close relatives of the Geiger family that lived along the Congaree River.

It was the morning of July 2, 1781; the siege of Ninety Six was still a searing wound. Colonel Cruger of the British forces was making his way to Orangeburg to join with Colonel Stuart and Lord Rawdon at Friday's Ferry at Fort Granby. General Nathanael Greene was attempting to strike Rawdon before he could join forces with Stuart and Cruger. Greene had sent couriers to Lee, Marion, Hampton, William Washington, Hill and Bratton to have them come to Granby. All but Sumter had been alerted.

Young Emily, being a loyal Patriot, asked if she could deliver the dispatch to General Sumter. She had often visited her relatives along the Congaree and knew the land well. Besides, a young girl could slip by unnoticed. Despite the danger, Greene set aside any doubt and sent Emily with the message to Sumter.

At Winnsboro, Greene briefed Emily on the contents of the message, helping her to commit it to memory. When she had traveled nearly five hours' distance

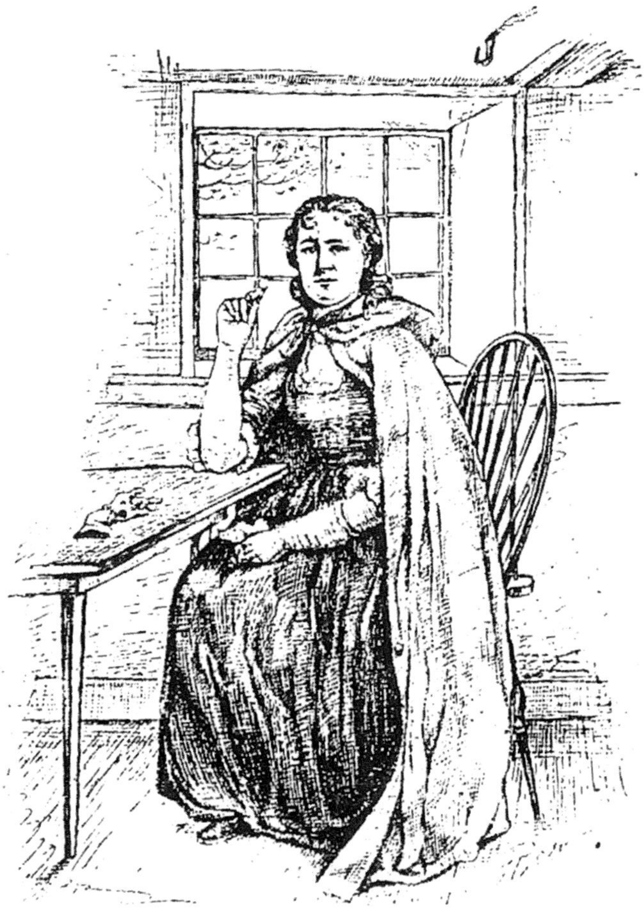

An illustration of Emily Geiger shown in *Harper's Weekly*.

from Greene's camp, a Tory spy, Bill Mink (Minick), learned of Emily's mission and set out upon her trail. As night fell on the first day's ride, Emily came upon a homestead and remained there for the rest of the night. Mink came upon the same homestead and asked of the planter, "Have you seen a slip of a girl, riding a small bay horse, pass during the afternoon?" The quick-witted Emily arose before dawn and changed her route to throw her tracker off her trail. She turned and crossed the Saluda at Lorrick's Ferry at Zion Church.

She had ridden some miles before being intercepted by three British soldiers from whom she learned that Rawdon had recaptured Fort Granby the night before. Thoroughly confusing her captors with her statements,

Emily was taken to Rawdon at the home of James Cayce at Fort Granby. While she was held in the southeastern room of the second story, awaiting a search by the wife and daughter of Tory leader Hogaboo, Emily swallowed the message, rendering the search fruitless. Emily was later escorted to the home of her uncle, Major Jacob Geiger, five miles below Granby.

Emily was free to complete her mission. With her cousin, she crossed the Congaree River at McCord's Ferry, and by midafternoon of the third day, on July 4, she found General Sumter's camp on the Wateree, where the road to Camden crossed, and delivered Greene's dispatch.

Although Greene failed in his original purpose, American troop movements forced Rawdon's early retreat toward Orangeburg, stopped Stuart's march and put Greene in possession of Fort Motte. The battle of Eutaw Springs came soon afterward and secured South Carolina for the Patriots.

Emily Geiger married Llewellyn Thurwitts of the Congarees and spent the remainder of her life at Granby and at the Patsy Jumper place ten miles below Columbia. It is said that Emily had a daughter, Emily Elizabeth, and perhaps a son. A Mrs. Buxton, of Vance's Ferry on the Santee, who claimed to be the daughter of Hogaboo, related to Benson Lossing in 1849 that Emily's daughter married her nephew, son of Peter Simons, and that Emily's daughter and Mr. Simons had a son who owned a plantation not far from Vance's Ferry.

Emily is buried in the Thurwitts family cemetery on the banks of Tom's Creek, where a stone marks her grave.

Tough "Old Sweet and Juicy"

Lyman Draper was a noted historian who chronicled the events of the American Revolution. His manuscripts can be found at the Wisconsin Historical Society. Draper received a letter from John Langford of Lexington County near Lorena, dated May 5, 1874, in which Mr. Langford goes into great detail about local Revolutionary War activities. Although John Langford was born in 1818, he personally knew many of the old folks who lived during the Revolution. One such character was James Calk, known as "Old Sweet and Juicy."

The story goes like this:

> *If I mistake not, the affair took place in the County of St. Matthews* [present Calhoun County]. *The command that he belonged to was attacked by a company of British. James and William Calk and their cousin Dixy Ward were taken prisoners, and were being conveyed to the British post at Monck's Corner. James Calk and the pony he was riding made such an unmilitary-like appearance he was not disarmed, and the prisoners, while marching along together were approached by the British captain, who rode up beside James Calk and began making fun of him by asking why such a tallow-faced fellow as he could do—he could not understand what sort of people the Americans were to put children and colts into the field expecting them to do proper service.*
>
> *Nettled by his insolence, young Calk instantly drew his sword and gave the Briton a blow just above the ear, laying him in the road weltering in his gore, while he, putting spurs to his pony, dashed through the guard and made his escape by lying down on his pony and galloping off under the old field pine limbs which hung so low to the ground that the British could not pursue him, and not thinking to shoot until he was fairly beyond their reach, he made his escape unhurt. His brother and the others made their escape that night, and if I mistake not, the captain was carried to Monck's Corner, and in time recovered.*
>
> *After the escape the Calks and their friends got together and came up the country and joined Captain Waters' Company of mounted rifles. That caused the Calks to be in the fight at the Weaver's Old Field between Colonel Hammond and Lord Rawdon's forces.*
>
> *After the war James Calk was a great hater of Tories, and had many sore combats with them, and sometimes being overpowered would get the worst of it. He was unconquerable as long as he lived.*

Hell Hole Massacre

Hell Hole, or Cloud's Creek, Massacre was an American Revolutionary War encounter in upper Lexington District. This massacre is sometimes referred to as the Turner House Massacre. This bloody event bears the epithet of Bloody Bill Cunningham, a murderous Tory if ever there was one.

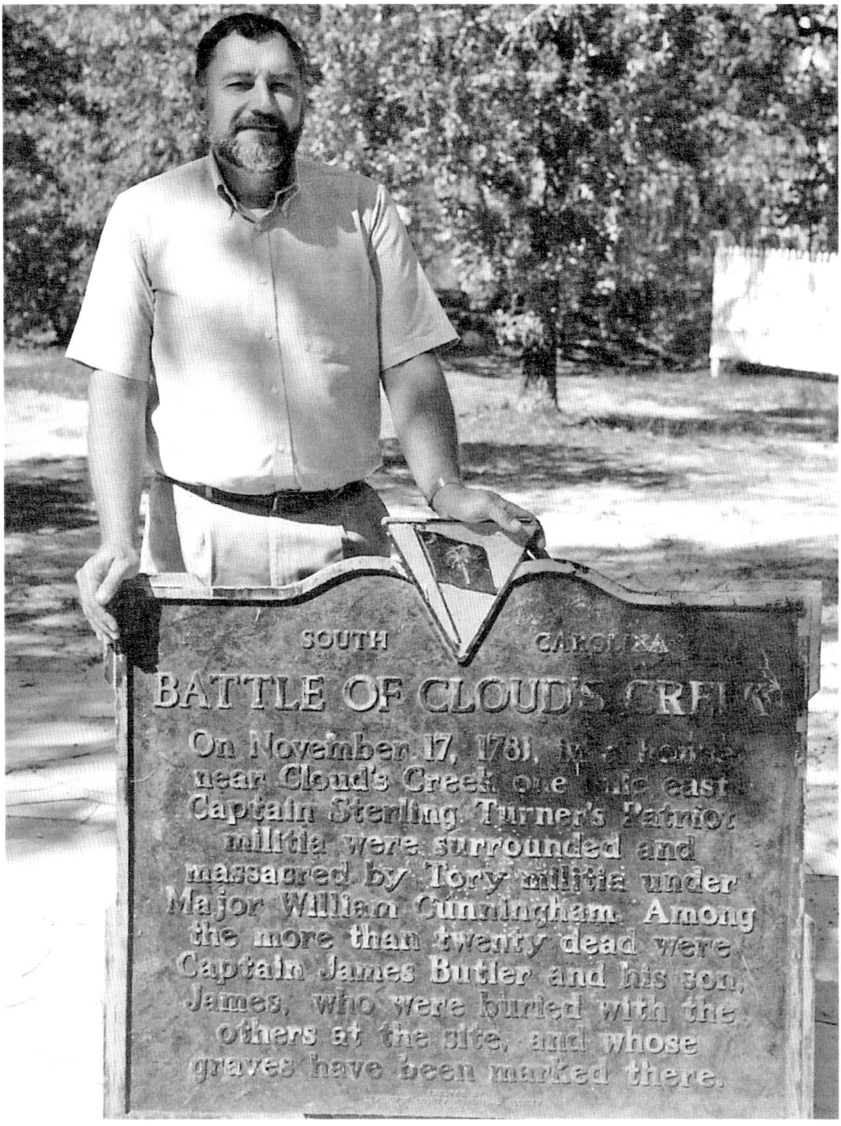

This marker of the Cloud's Creek Massacre has been removed by vandals several times and is now at the Lexington County Museum. Shown with the marker is Horace Harmon, retired curator of Lexington County Museum.

In a span of a few short weeks, Bloody Bill and his marauding band of Tories killed many Patriots from Anderson's Mill on the Upper Saluda to Cloud's Creek on the Lower Saluda, literally leaving the country through which they passed in tears.

Cunningham detached a party of about 300 mounted men from Lord Rawdon's British forces to pursue Colonel Samuel Hammond of Edgefield. Having missed Hammond at Anderson's Mill, Bloody Bill made his way to Cloud's Creek, where Mount Willing Road crossed the Little Saluda River. All along his path, Cunningham left bloodstained homesteads and burning houses. On November 8, 1781, Bloody Bill arrived at Hollow Creek with 150 men and promptly engaged a party of Patriots looking to retrieve stolen livestock from British troops.

This small party of twenty-two volunteers was led by Captain James Turner. Captain Sterling Butler also joined the party to assist in the search. They had been out in a hard rain all day and had taken refuge in the unfortified Turner House. Cunningham was informed as to their whereabouts by an escaped Tory prisoner by the name of George Martin Caughman. As Turner, Butler and the twenty-two volunteers took cover at the house, Cunningham attacked. With little ammunition and wet weapons, and being greatly outnumbered, the Patriots soon surrendered. A promise of kind treatment and prisoner of war status was requested, but none was given. As Turner, Butler and their men surrendered, they met with Bloody Bill's lust for slaughter. Butler's twelve-year-old son was among those surrendering. Butler pleaded for the boy's freedom in exchange for his own unconditional surrender, but his pleas went unheeded. Butler's son lies buried with the rest of the Patriots in this hell hole.

The story of the massacre was told by H. Arthur Fort in the Draper manuscripts:

> *Nathaniel Corley, a large and strong man, drew his sword and tried to cut his way through the line. He almost got to his horse when a volley broke his thigh. As he reached for his horse's tail another volley fired, killing him.*
>
> *The sole survivor, Benjamin Hughes, escaped by bolting through a cow pen. James "Old Sweet & Juicy" Calk and few other men went after the murdering Tories in hot pursuit, catching up with them at the Enoree River near Newberry. He made the rascals "smell the potching." In other words, he shot them point blank for their misdeeds at the Lick. Those who were not killed were brought back to Cloud's Creek and hung near Cedar Grove Church in Lexington County.*
>
> *Colonel Hammond was at the Turner House the following day and described a heart-rending scene of women burying the mutilated bodies of their dead husbands, fathers, and brothers.*
>
> *Bloody Bill Cunningham escaped to fight another day, but the American Revolution was over.*

Bloody Bill Cunningham

Tory Bandit

The Cunningham family moved to the Ninety Six District from Virginia some time during the 1750s. Young William was a lively, jovial and generous young man with a quick and fiery temper. He was a remarkable horseman who loved the finer things in life. Because of this, he was a favorite of the young people in his neighborhood. At the beginning of the American Revolution, in 1776, young Cunningham was struggling with his politics but was leaning toward the Whigs.

Later, this same spirited young man became the despised Bloody Bill Cunningham, remembered for atrocities committed against fellow countrymen at Anderson's Mill, Cloud's Creek and Hayes' Station.

History remembers the incidents that led to this turn of events. But if the events had not turned Cunningham, his family surely would have, for they were officers in the Loyalist militia. Robert, David and Patrick Cunningham all remained loyal to the British Crown.

Cunningham's first dispute with the Whigs came from Captain John Caldwell. Cunningham had served under Caldwell at the beginning of the Revolution and had been promised a commission and a guarantee that he would not have to serve in Charleston. Eventually, Cunningham was ordered to Charleston, at which point he resigned, along with the troops he had brought into Caldwell's company. Caldwell was none too pleased and had the young Cunningham arrested and tried for mutiny. Cunningham was acquitted of the charges and returned to the backcountry, where he once again served with the Patriots under General Williams in his struggles with the Cherokee Campaign.

In 1778, Cunningham went to Savannah at the urging of his family. While there, a gang led by his sworn enemy, Captain William Ritchie, whipped to death Cunningham's lame and epileptic brother, John. Cunningham set out on foot to avenge his brother's death. Ritchie and his men were gathered outside when Cunningham was spotted walking toward them. Ritchie uttered, "Lord have mercy on me, for yonder is young Cunningham and I am a dead man." And indeed, Cunningham shot Ritchie as he was making his escape. As Cunningham drew close to the dying man he said, "I have come all the way

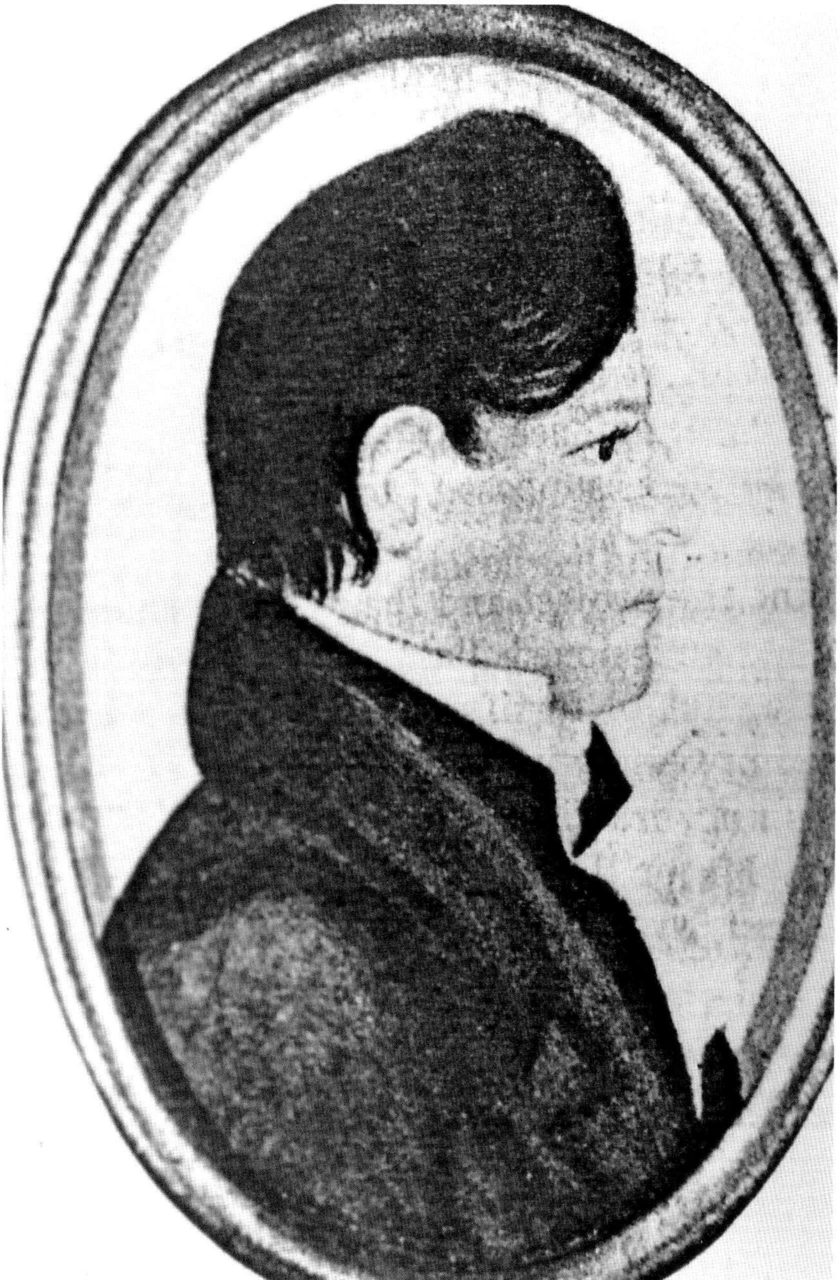

William Cunningham, alias Bloody Bill.

from Savannah on foot to kill you for the crimes you have committed against my family." This episode sealed the fate of William Cunningham.

As a British officer, Cunningham rose rapidly to the rank of major. He vigorously enforced Cornwallis's order to execute all rebels who refused to pledge allegiance to the Crown. Easily earning the name Bloody Bill, Cunningham and his desperate gang of highway robbers began their bloody rampage through the backcountry of South Carolina at Anderson's Mill on the upper Saluda River, leaving a trail of blood and tears that is remembered to this day.

After Anderson's Mill, Cunningham next appeared in Lexington District at Cloud's Creek, where his gang massacred twenty-two of the district's citizens, including two of the Butler family. Cunningham's next victim was Major John Caldwell, an uncle of John C. Calhoun. From there he went to Hayes' Station, where he butchered Colonel Joseph Hayes, Captain Daniel Williams, Lieutenant Christopher Hardy, Lieutenant John Neil, Clement Hancock, Joseph Williams, Joseph Irby Sr., Joseph Irby Jr., John Milvin, James Feris, John Cook, Greaf Irby, Benjamin Goodman, Yancy Saxon, Captain Owens and Captain Leonard—all without mercy.

William Lee, a notorious bandit, had joined Cunningham's band, and the South Carolina Senate created a special company of rangers to capture Cunningham and Lee, offering a reward—dead or alive. The senate labeled Cunningham one of the "most noted of the banditti who have so long infested the district of Ninety Six."

Cunningham made his way back to the Lowcountry, but in the process he lost his beloved mare, Ringtail (Silver Heels). The thoroughbred mare had rescued Cunningham many times when pursued by less fleet-footed steed. The long chase through the backcountry proved too much for her, and she died within days of their return to Charleston.

As the British retreated from Charleston, Cunningham took refuge in East Florida, eventually going into exile in Nassau, Bahamas. In 1782, the General Assembly confiscated his property, and on January 20, 1787, the notorious Bloody Bill Cunningham died in Nassau.

The Cunningham Legacy

Local history, with or without the aid of genealogy, can answer a lot of questions about family history. A search of the local library can yield abundant information about a family tree. Voices calling in the blood are responsible for hordes of pilgrims staring blankly, eyes bulging from information-highway fatigue.

Centuries separate us from our ancestral homelands. Flood, fire, wind and war, along with forgetfulness, have done immense damage to our collective history. But still they come, those diligent workers, gathering and collecting pieces of the past.

The work of the local historian is not without its reward. The craft of preserving the story of a community connects you with your own story, and in doing so you discover your own uniqueness through the study of generations of your own family.

The resurgence of historical rediscovery has germinated in the fertile ground of the Southern parlor, where ancestor worship has been dutifully nurtured into an art form and genealogical voyeurism is more entertaining than a good mystery.

Local history is full of paradox. Fiction pales in comparison to true accounts of villainy and sainthood found in the legends and recollections of local histories. Personalities endure for generations, and none more than that of William "Bloody Bill" Cunningham, the ruthless and wanton Tory of the American Revolutionary War.

Bloody Bill took every opportunity to shoot, hang and slash the enemies of King George throughout Orangeburg District and the Carolina backcountry. He was never caught or punished for his murderous ways, but he died in exile, a still young—but broken—man.

At war's end, Bloody Bill and his Loyalist cousins, Patrick and Robert, were driven out of South Carolina. Bloody Bill and Robert died in Nassau. Patrick Cunningham, however, lived and petitioned the newly formed American government to be allowed back into the country. His petition was initially denied, but a second request proved successful. Patrick, his wife and children were allowed to return to Laurens County, where they reclaimed some of their confiscated lands and lost Cunningham family reputation.

It was Patrick's granddaughter, Ann Pamela Cunningham, who eventually restored the jewel in the Cunningham family crown. Ann Pamela Cunningham, an invalid, worked tirelessly to found the Mount Vernon Association, which bought and restored Mount Vernon, the home of George Washington.

How ironic that the same family that declared its allegiance to the Crown also saved the home of the commander in chief of American forces and first president of the United States.

George Washington Comes Calling

At 6:00 a.m. on the morning of May 21, 1791, Colonel Thomas Taylor, Colonel Wade Hampton, R. Lythroe and Mr. Jameson arrived in Augusta to escort President George Washington to Columbia. The escort party arrived at Granby with the president at sunset the next day.

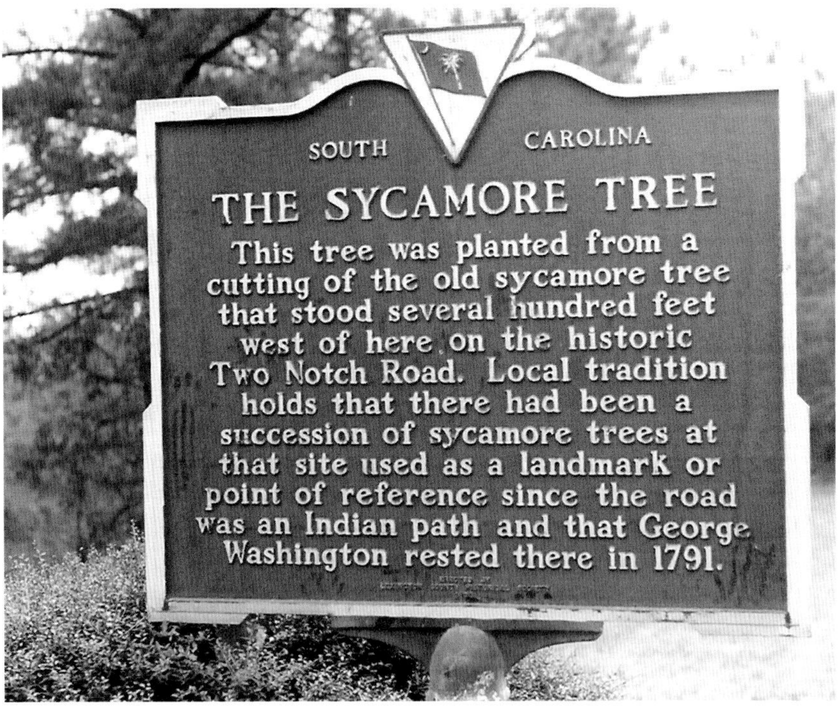

A marker placed at the site of the original sycamore tree along U.S. Highway 1 in Lexington County.

The people of the community were lined along the riverbank when the party arrived, hoping to catch a glimpse of the president as he crossed the river at Friday's Ferry. Only months before, the Hamptons had begun building a toll bridge at the site. Heavy rains had washed the bridge away, and there had not been time to rebuild it before the president's arrival.

George Washington crossed the Congaree River at Friday's Ferry and was greeted on the eastern shore by a contingency of officers led by Captain Kershaw. Washington was escorted to a local home, where a reception had been prepared for him. Here he was introduced to his escort troop and the gentlemen of Columbia.

Washington recorded the day's events in his diary:

> **Sunday, 22nd** *Rode twenty-one miles to breakfast, and passing through the village of Granby, just below the falls in the Congaree (which was passed in a flat bottom boat at a rope ferry) I lodged at Columbia, the newly adopted seat of government of South Carolina about three miles from it, on the north side of the river, and twenty-seven from my breakfasting stage.*
> **Tuesday, 24th** *Columbia is laid out upon a large scale; but in my opinion, had better been placed on the river below the falls. It is now an uncleared wood, with very few houses in it, and those all wooden. The State House (which is also of wood) is a large and commodious building, but unfinished. The Town is on dry, but cannot be called high ground, and though surrounded by Piney and Sandy land is, itself good. The State House is near two miles from the river, at the confluence of the Broad River and Saluda. From Granby the river is navigable for craft which will, when the river is a little swelled, carry over 3,000 bushels of grain—when at its usual height less, and always some. The river from hence to the Wateree, below which takes the name of Santee, is very crooked; it being according to the computed distance nearly 400 miles—Columbia from Charleston is one hundred and thirty miles.*

Washington made a practice not to stop at private homes along this route. Although it is not known for certain where Washington lodged in Columbia, some believe he stayed at the inn belonging to Colonel Thomas Taylor. Washington traveled in a chariot pulled by four horses. The refurbished coach was painted white, with decorative embellishments and gilded framework and springs. A valet, two footmen, a coachman and postilion and five saddle horses accompanied him.

Colonel Thomas Taylor, leader of his escort from Augusta, was one of the region's most influential citizens. Taylor was the eldest son of John Taylor, who brought his family from Virginia to Black Swamp in 1750. The Taylor home, Taylor's Hill, was at the corner of Barnwell and Richland Streets. Taylor served as justice of the peace for Kershaw District and was a member of the first and second provincial congress. He later served as a state senator and as a member of the national congress. He was also a founding member of the First Presbyterian Church in Columbia.

At noon on May 23, a large crowd of 130 people from Granby, Winnsboro, Camden, Stateburg, Bellville, Orangeburg and surrounding countryside began arriving for a reception at the hall of the House of Representatives, where Washington was introduced to 60 of Columbia's ladies. From here, guests went to the senate room, where they enjoyed a plentiful dinner. Although Martha Washington did not travel with the president, Lady Street was named in honor of the first lady.

The occasion was a happy one, and many toasts were made. They were made to the United States, to the state of South Carolina, to the twenty-third of May, to the memory of General Greene and Justice Pendleton, to sufficient means and speedy measure for opening the inland navigation of America, to the farmers, manufacturers and merchants of America—may their well-directed exertions reward their industry.

Later in the evening, a ball was held at the Assembly Hall. Washington was quite fond of dancing and danced well into the evening. Washington remained in Columbia a day longer than he had planned because of a lame horse, but no public events were held that day.

When he departed, Washington acknowledged Columbia's warm hospitality by saying:

> *I am much obliged by your professions of respect and affection, and I am truly grateful for your kind regards and good wishes. I desire to assure you that I shall always remember with pleasure your polite attention.*

After leaving Columbia, Washington traveled on to Camden.

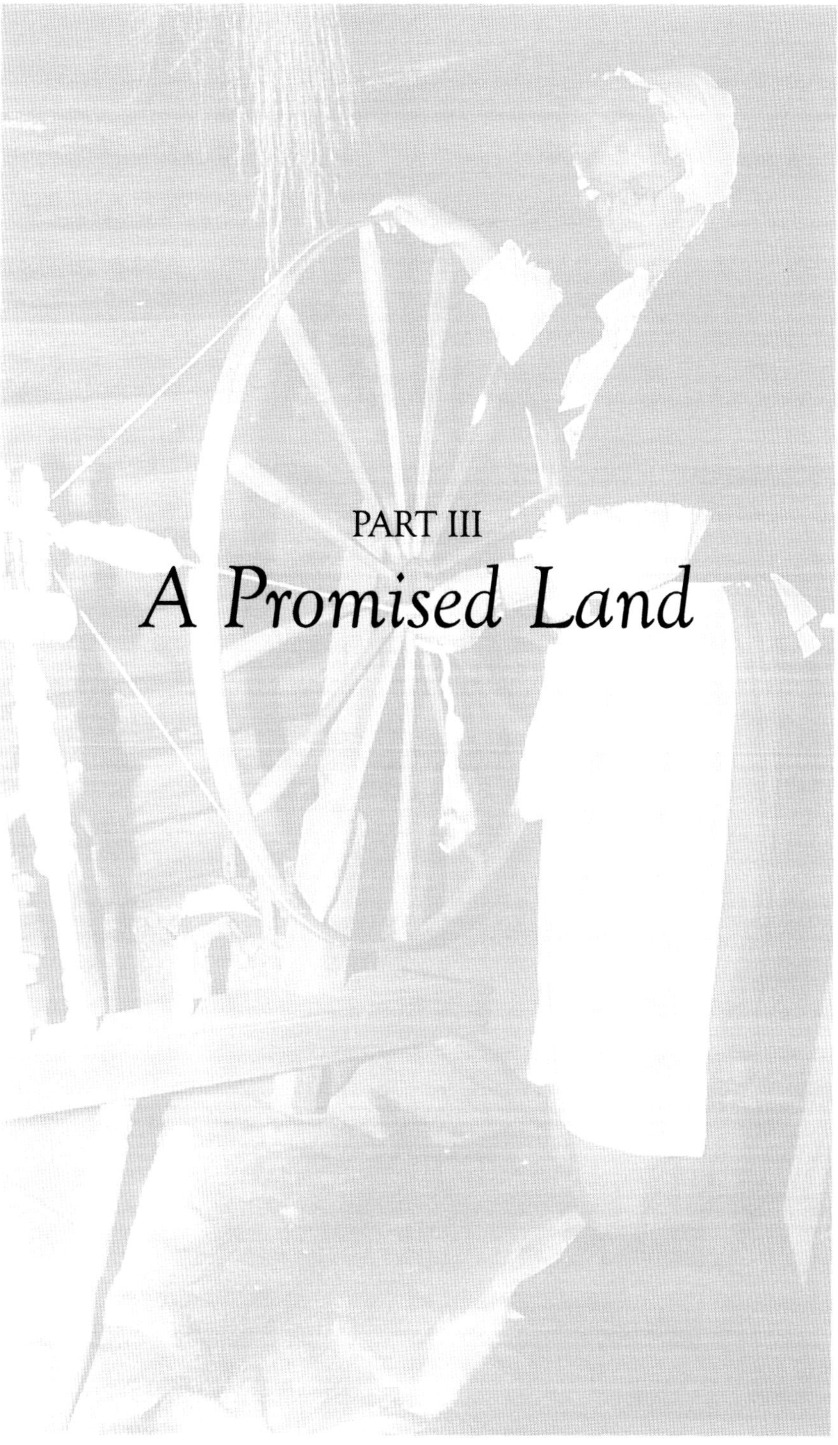

PART III
A Promised Land

A Settlement Flowing with Milk and Honey

"Taking tea, coffee, and medicine was nothing but pride," said Andrew Tarrer. His diet consisted of soup in the morning and milk in the evening because he "never needed anything else."

Andrew Tarrer's evening summer drink was probably clabber or buttermilk he kept in the springhouse or his summer dairy. The summer dairy sat off the ground about three feet and had a hinged door. His winter dairy was similar, but with ventilation slats. Milk was by far the favored drink of his community. For special occasions there was apple cider, persimmon beer, peach brandy and wine made from native fruits, berries and grapes. Peaches were so plentiful that many were fed to the hogs. Sweetened tea became a favorite much later.

According to William Summer, sauerkraut was the national dish of the Dutch Fork. It was cooked with pork ribs or backbone and served with dip dumplings. The main meal of the day was served at noon. The farmer's wife called field hands in with a cow horn—a tradition brought from Europe.

Pork, mutton, poultry and beef were preferred meats. But the German farmer always had his rabbit boxes set and was an excellent hunter. The occasional cooter found at the creek was always a cause for jubilation at the dinner table. Meats were cooked over the hearth fire or in spider ovens that sat among the hot coals and contained deep-dish meat pies or pastry-filled stews. A favorite stew was liver nips, which was made by grinding liver and then mixing in flour, eggs, suet, onions and seasonings. The dumplings then would be dropped by the spoonful into boiling beef stock.

Fruit pies were served as sweets. Stewed apples folded into saucer-shaped pastry and deep fried were sure to please. Seasonal vegetables were plentiful, with a mixture of German, African and native varieties. Hop vines were a necessity in the garden. Hop dust was used to make rising powder by pouring boiling water over the hop flowers and then adding cornmeal to the strained and dried hops. The dried powder was stored for later use. As an alternative, Irish potatoes were used to make liquid yeast for sourdough bread.

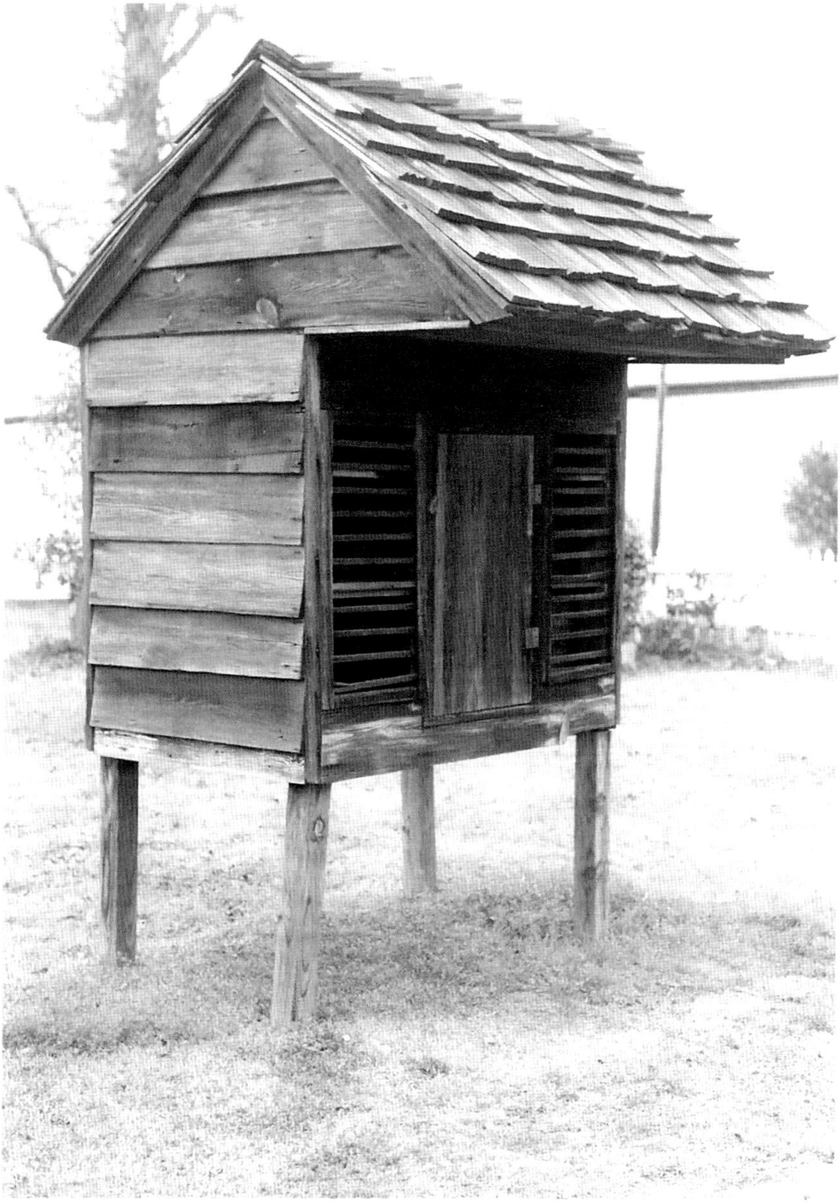

In a time before refrigeration, milk and eggs were kept in a dairy such as this.

Dutch Ovens of Switzers' Neck

We thought Grandma Minnie was not quite right when she asked Grandpa to bring the old wood stove back into the house from the barn, where it had been stored. Grandma had been happy cooking with gas, but as the years wore on the lure of the old wood stove won out. She preferred the old way of cooking. So it has been with the "Dutch" housewife for generations.

The Swiss/German housewife was noted for her cooking. She had many new foods at her disposal, in addition to ones she brought with her from the Rhinelands.

In the early years of frontier settlement, bread, pies, puddings, sweet potatoes and roasted peanuts were baked in igloo-shaped outdoor ovens. The first ovens were built of stone and clay and later were made with sundried bricks and mortar. Ovens stood four to five feet tall and would hold a week's supply of baked goods at one firing. This style of bake oven was common in the Black Forest of Bavaria.

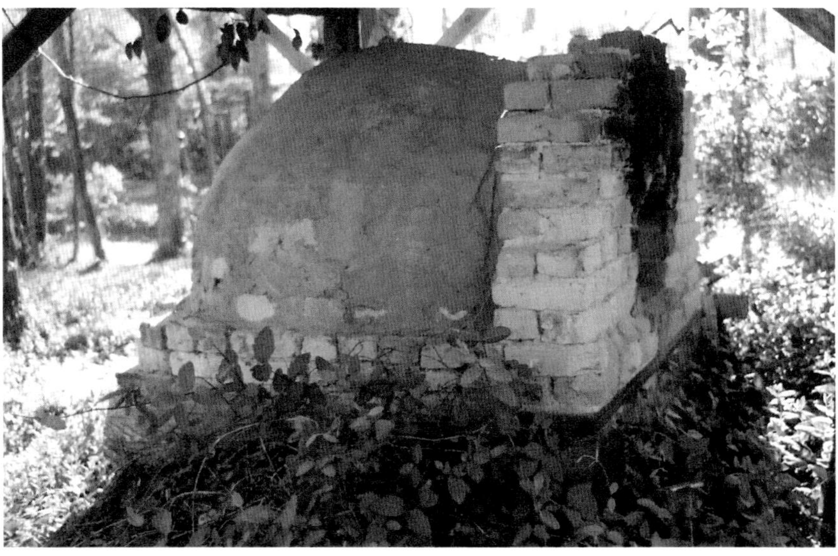

This Dutch oven was once used to bake bread, pies and cakes in Lexington.

A shed covered the cooking area to prevent a sudden rain from cooling the oven and drenching the baker. A small arched opening allowed ample access and contained the heat behind a metal door. To get the bricks hot enough for baking, a fire was built in the center of the oven using broken fence rails, tanning bars and cobs. When the desired temperature was reached, an oak leaf placed inside the oven would curl. The hot coals were raked down and covered with tin, the vent was plugged and the oven was ready for its delectable edibles. The oven was fired up once or twice a week, depending on the family's needs. In 1930, Clayton Kleckley, family historian, recollected that the ladies of Switzers' Neck abandoned their modern kitchens to bake a batch of Christmas fruitcakes. And you know Grandma Minnie, a young mother at the time, was probably right in the midst of it all.

Herbs for Healing, Eating and Drinking

With drugstores practically on every corner today, it is hard to imagine how folks survived without modern-day merchandising. The settlers of Saxe Gotha Township turned to the woodlands and their own knowledge of herbs and medicine that they brought with them to the frontier. They grew and gathered plants to flavor sausages, treat ailments or to make teas and wines. Many plants served a dual purpose.

Rosemary, sage, mint, basil, parsley and garlic were passed down among family, friends and neighbors. Plant starts were customarily given to newlyweds as wedding gifts. Teas made from red pepper, dogwood bark, pine tops and wild mullein were brewed as a cure for chills. Beargrass boiled in sweet cream was used in a poultice for poison ivy. Sweet shrub twigs boiled into tea were used to treat measles. The "Dutch" housewife used bandages soaked in a brew made from white lily petals steeped in whiskey to heal a wound or cut. Silkwood tea was considered a cure for rheumatism.

Dr. Orlando Benedict Mayer was known to have prescribed asafetida (essafittity) for hysterics. "Give her plenty of essafittity, tell her mammy to

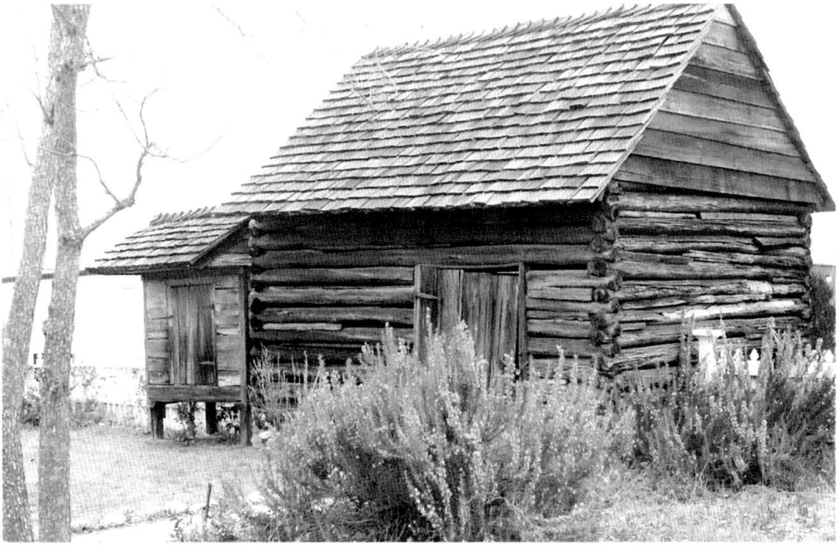

Herbs were grown by the Dutch housewife for cooking and medicines.

whip her three times a day, and keep her continerly at the spinnin' wheel." Essafittity powder sacks were also worn around the neck for inhaling as a preventative.

The common dandelion was brought here from Europe and cultivated as a garden plant. The tousle-headed weed we know today escaped these early confines and naturalized. The dandelion puffball was multipurpose: it was used to tell the weather, predict the outcome of a love match and send loving thoughts. To dream of a dandelion was said to foretell misfortune and treachery on the part of a loved one. During the Civil War, roasted dandelion root was used as a coffee substitute. It is one European plant that Native Americans readily adopted.

In the early nineteenth century, clothing was made from materials grown, dyed, spun and woven in the home. Yarns were dipped in dye pots filled with boiling liquids made with black walnut hulls, onion skins and sumac bark. Powdered madder root produced a prized red, while parsley, indigo and maple bark produced blues and greens. These enduring fabrics made by early German homemakers can still be found in the Dutch Fork some two centuries later, attesting to their skills in cloth making and the durability of their product.

John Adam Summer

Early Dutch Fork Settler

How John Adam Summer came to the Dutch Fork area is a tale of adventure. As O.B. Mayer tells us, he gathered many truthful records to

> *establish facts, write out an inferential narrative exquisitely romantic, which however improbable it may seem here and there, must be accepted as true, because the preponderance of truth usually converts improbability into fact and absorbs it.*

With that said, let us proceed with the story of John Adam Summer.

John Adam Summer was born in the Oldenwald Mountains of southern Germany, near Wurtenburg. For centuries, Germany's peasants were under siege by potentates. Large numbers of people were forced into service or voluntarily served as mercenaries in the armies of these princes. Because of this practice, many of Germany's peasants fled to the New World. Adam Summer was one of these emigrants who worked off his passage to the New World on a Dutch galleon.

Between 1735 and 1740, he arrived in New York, where he was told he would find large colonies of Germans in Pennsylvania. Summer moved on to Pennsylvania, where he became friends with an American Indian boy. The two young adventurers went on many expeditions together, and Summer became a trusted ally of many tribes.

In time, Summer heard more tales of white settlers farther to the south with many Germans among them. Summer then made plans to travel south to Georgia. His Native American friends unsuccessfully tried to dissuade him from leaving, but he did agree to delay his journey for ten days at their request.

The mystery of the ten-day delay was solved on Summer's second day on the trail. A message from his old friend had been sent ahead from tribe to tribe with instructions to assist Summer along his way through Maryland, Virginia and North Carolina. Finally, under the guidance of the Catawba tribe, he reached Ruff's Mountain, where he crossed the Broad River and traveled along Crim's Creek. It is said that the stone hills of Lexington so reminded Summer of the Oldenwald Mountains and the Rhine Valley that he decided to make the little mountain his permanent home. Summer returned to Pennsylvania to let others know of his discovery, and many came south with him to the Dutch Fork.

Orlando Benedict Mayer on the Dutch Fork

Orlando Benedict Mayer lived and wrote in the Dutch Fork during the nineteenth century. It was his desire to illustrate and recall the manners and customs of this community of people. In the last four months of his life in 1891, Mayer published *The Dutch Fork* in eleven serial installments in the *Newberry Herald and News*.

Mayer warned his readers that he sometimes "departs from the mere facts," and used creativity to entertain and teach. The following is an excerpt from "A Stroll in Dutch Fork":

> *After the confirmation of Molly's story, I had no doubt that it (a thing, which had the body of a Billy goat and the head of a man which was heard to grunt and sneeze like a person having a bad cold) was the ghost of Old Shumpert she had seen. I had often heard of his appearing to people in the shape of*

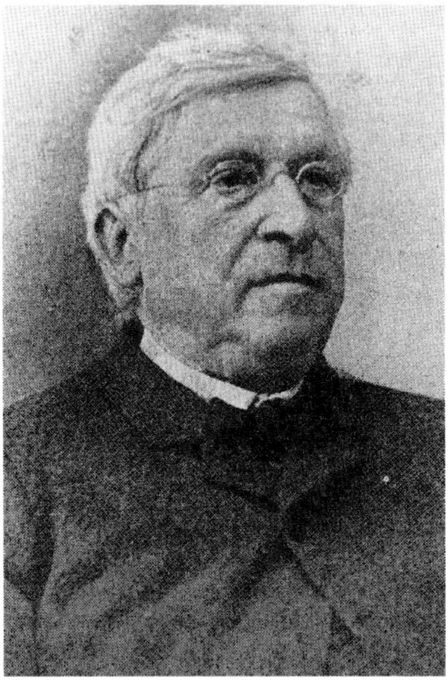

O.B. Mayer of the Dutch Fork wrote about the people and customs of his community.

different animals. I recollected with horror, how he encountered Betty Fry once, in open daylight, looking like a hog that had been scalded and scrapped; and running after her with its throat cut from ear to ear, and its liver and lights, et cetera, trailing along behind it.

…The situation of the thing *was now critical in the extreme, and it certainly would have been excused for attempting to escape; but no—it stood perfectly still, and just as the allied forces rushed upon it, (nobody but Old Shumpert could have done it) changed itself into as ordinary a lightwood stump as I ever saw. He was so hard pressed that he was compelled to change himself into an object, against which there was no counter-metamorphosis, at least, so the legend goes.*

Granny Summer

Although the stories of Orlando B. Mayer appeared in print only a short time, they left a lasting impression of the Dutch Fork's quaint customs upon the reader. In a passage from "A Stroll in Dutch Fork," Mayer managed to leave us with a shimmering glimpse of Granny Summer and her house filled with merriment.

We call her Granny Summer. Heaven bless her goodness of heart, and let her abundant charity cover a multitude of sins. Granny Summer was a user—one who cures many diseases, especially diseases of the eye, by a species of sorcery called using.

Granny Summer would trace the point of one finger around the eye and repeat, in a low tone in German, the following incantation: "The slear is the dragon, went together over the brook. The slear was drowned, and the dragon disappeared, God the Father, God the Son, and God the Holy Ghost. Amen." The slear is the name given to an inflammation. Early in the morning the patient was taken to a stream and the user, dipping water over the inflammation, recited the incantation.

I looked upon the old house and thought of the time when I was present at a tremendous wedding…what jollification there was in the house, when the young people danced with a vigor that made it dangerous for persons of delicate health to be near them, and above the din of the crowded reel could be heard the foot of Sligh's Bob, the fiddler, beating time, but absolutely crushing it into chaos.

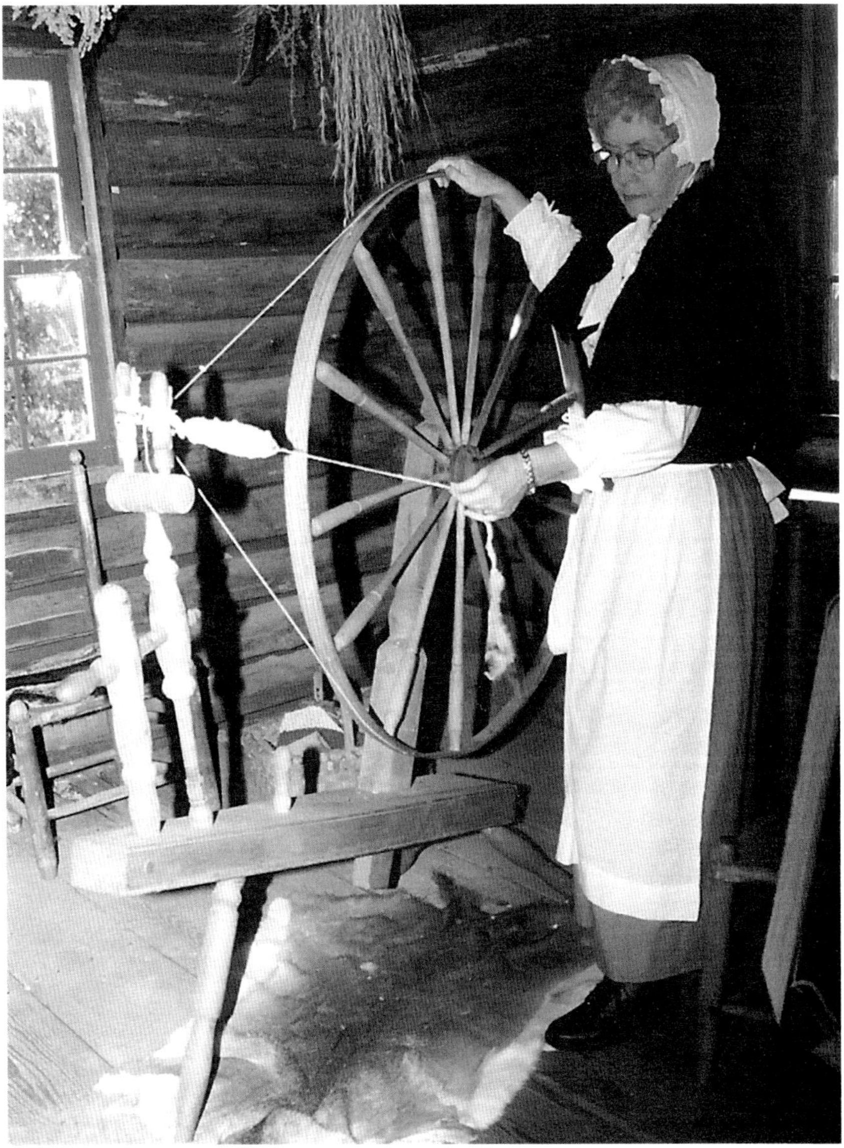

Spinning wheels such as this provided yarns for clothing the backcountry family.

I can see myself peeping through the fence at the many twinkling feet, reliving the astonishment I felt at Tom Sligh who sprang incessantly into the air, crossing his legs three times before retouching the floor to the tune of "Rip tip tido, Kate's Got a Man."

But the old house is passing away. It has grown gray with mildew and lichen, and rain which once pounded the eaves in such glittering fingers is now absorbed through the swollen shingles, and drips its midnight monody upon the floor.

Easter Traditions of the German Settlers

Katie Monts related Easter traditions of the German settlers of Lexington County:

I learned to save a patch from every calico dress. At Easter I sewed these patches around the eggs very tightly and put these to boil with a shovel of wood ash thrown in the water. When the patches dried I cut them off and the designs were there beautifully.

Easter was a very big religious celebration, bigger even than Christmas. The entire family always attended preaching on Good Friday and Easter Sunday. Holy Thursday, or Green Thursday, and Easter Monday were also included in the holy days of Easter.

Eggs played an important part in the celebrations, especially among the children. Several weeks before Easter, the children began collecting eggs for dyeing on the Saturday before Easter Sunday. Eggs were dyed by boiling them in a spider oven set among the hot coals of the hearth fire. Most eggs were dyed red, using madder; some were dyed purple, using logwood; and some were dyed yellow, using tea and broom sedge.

The eggs were decorated with pictures, verses and the names of those to whom they were being given by scratching a design on the shell with a knife. It was the custom in southern Germany and Switzerland to give decorated eggs as a token of friendship.

There was also the custom of pecking or *eirspecken*, in which the ends of two eggs were struck together by a pair of opponents. Mr. J.M. Eleazer explained the game this way:

> *We played a game of chance with 'em. Peckin' eggs, we called it. You'd banter another kid to peck with you. You'd hold your egg concealed in your hand with only a bit of one end showing between your thumb and forefinger. The other fellow would hit one of his eggs against it. The egg that broke went to the winner. After winning a broken egg, we'd eat it.*

Rabbit nests were also a big part of Easter celebrations. This tradition, although common in Lexington, was little known outside this and other German settlements and the German district of Swabia. The Easter Rabbit and his eggs were first seen in Germany in the 1500s. The children made rabbit nests on the Saturday before Easter by digging shallow holes in the ground and lining them with grass and flowers. Katie Monts recollected, "Our rabbit nests were always made in the lilies, which grew in the garden. Our parents insisted that we make them there because dogs would eat the eggs if they were laid outside."

Traditions of egg dyeing, pecking, decorating and hiding eggs were unique to our German community, but later became widespread throughout America in the twentieth century.

English Comes to the Dutch Fork

The year was 1814. Most of the Dutch Fork and Switzers' Neck all the way to Saxe Gotha spoke the German language in their homes, churches and schools. Even those who had slaves taught them the tongue of the old country. This was a time of transition. The younger people, those born in America, wanted to speak English. During this time, the early Reformed ministers were dying out and American Lutheran seminaries were providing a new supply of ministers. The Reverend Joseph Wallern of Newberry District was the last surviving minister of the Unis Ecclesiastica, which was formed some thirty years earlier at Zion Church.

Bethel Church at High Hill was one of the first churches to change to English, and was soon joined by several members from Zion. This group later became St. Michael's Church, with Godfrey Dreher as its minister, and was part of the North Carolina Synod. The first communion in English was given on October 18, 1814.

In the spring of 1816, the Lutheran Church in South Carolina held its first ecclesiastical conference at Bethel Church. The Reverends Charles Stork and R.J. Miller opened the conference in English, while Godfrey Dreher and Michael Rauch addressed English visitors outdoors. On the second day of the conference, the Reverend Shobler delivered his sermon in German and addressed the Negroes on Christianity. Another meeting was held at St. Michael's the following Monday at 9:00 a.m.

The purpose of the conference was to address several issues that had arisen with the growth of Lutheranism. It was decided at the conference that children of unworthy members, who were not expelled, could be presented in the church by their own parents, provided worthy members acted as sponsors, presenting them at the altar.

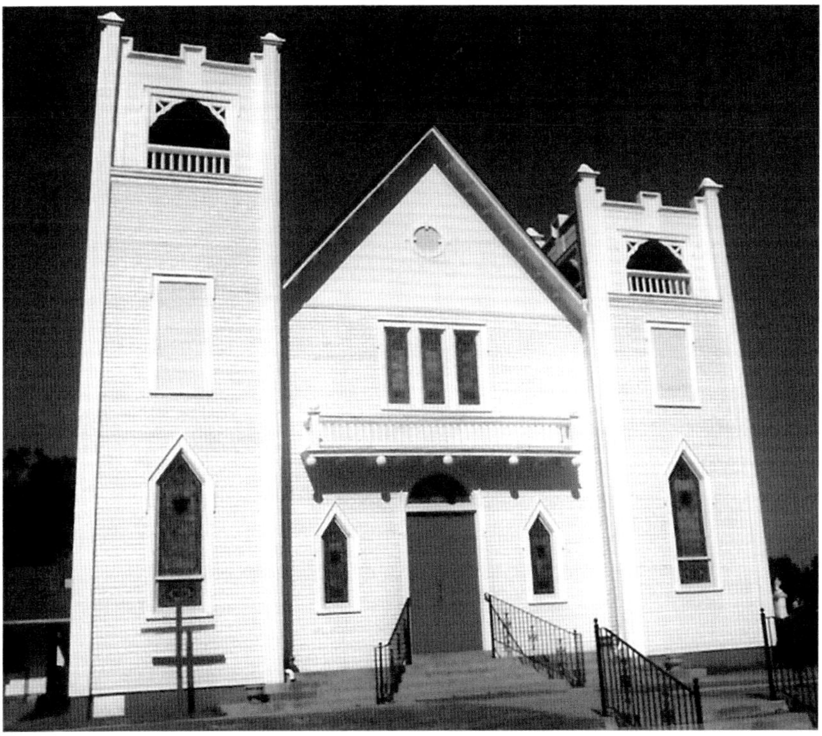

St. Michael's Lutheran Church was one of the first churches of the Dutch Fork.

Other issues concerned its slave membership. The question was raised as to whether a slave should be confirmed or baptized, and whether he or she should serve a probation period before being allowed to take communion. The conference also questioned whether slaves should be at liberty to choose a church or attend the same church as their masters. The marriage bond was also recognized and strictly enforced.

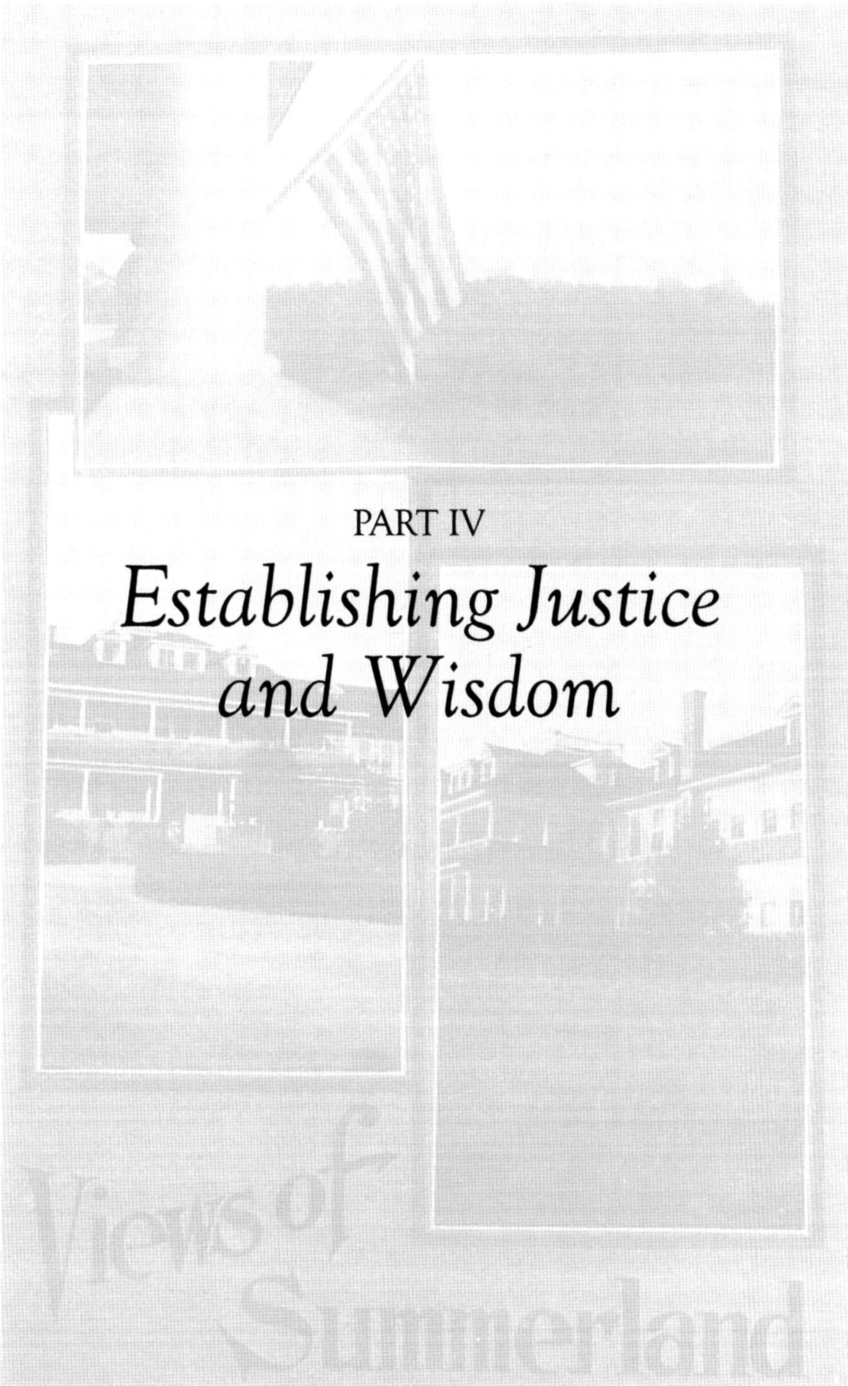

PART IV
Establishing Justice and Wisdom

Lexington Courthouse

In 1820, the town of Lexington became the county seat. Granby, the former county seat, was located across the Congaree River from the new state capital, Columbia. Granby Courthouse was moved to Columbia. It was used by First Presbyterian Church and later as a residence. It is no longer standing.

Practically all of Lexington was right square in the middle of Laurance Corley's plantation. Corley, a Patriot of the American Revolution, lived only a short while after the county seat was moved to Lexington. His second wife and widow, Granny Barbara Drafts Corley, built the first house in Lexington along its main street on the southeastern corner of Main and South Lake Drive.

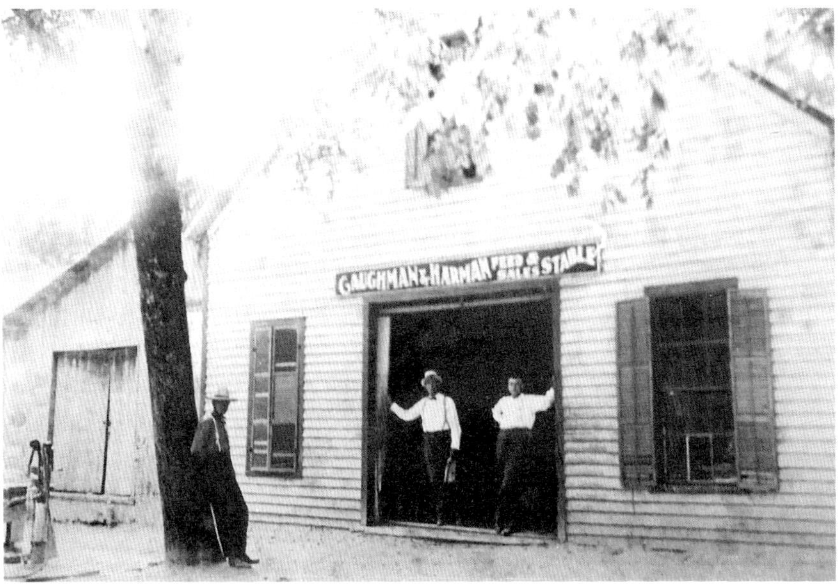

The Caughman and Harman Livery Stable in early Lexington near the courthouse.

In 1839, a stately antebellum courthouse was built on the northwestern corner of Main Street. Sherman burned this courthouse in 1865. A wooden courthouse was built in 1866 at this site. It was torn down in 1881.

In 1882, another courthouse was built at the same site. This structure was brick and was demolished in 1955. Another courthouse was completed in 1940, and a new courthouse was built in 2003.

Advocates of Free Education

Churches held communities together on the frontier. They provided shelter from danger, a gathering place and a place to nourish the spirit and mind.

Early ministers often had an enduring influence on their flocks. The Reverend Christian Theus was one of these ministers who served as teacher and shepherd. Abraham Geiger of Zion Church in the Switzers' Neck was

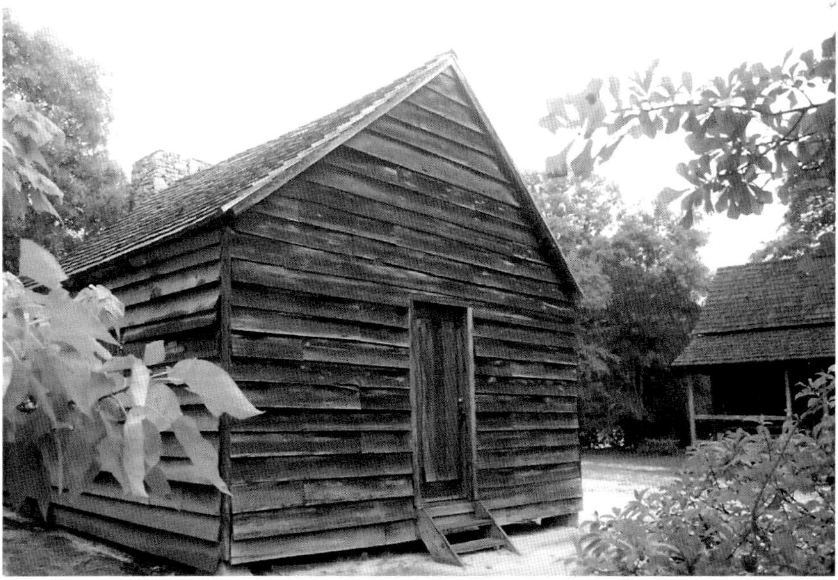

An old field school built prior to the Civil War. This school can be seen at the Lexington County Museum.

a friend and ally of the Reverend Theus. Geiger recorded his loyalty to the faithful minister on Theus's tombstone: "This faithful divine labored through a long life as a faithful servant in his Master's vineyard, and the reward which he received from the many for his labor was ingratitude."

Perhaps the Reverend Theus inspired Geiger's loyalty by providing the special education he needed as a child handicapped by smallpox. Despite his handicap, Geiger learned and prospered. At his death, he was the wealthiest man in the Congarees. Geiger excelled as an agriculturist, developed vineyards, served in public office and established the Platt Springs Academy that was well-known for many years as one of the state's finest preparatory schools.

Geiger supported the school primarily from his own funds that were raised from his agricultural and business pursuits. The center of his operations was Poor Hope, his plantation in Gaston, where he managed a winery, vineyards, cotton gin and press, a warehouse and a mill.

Abraham Geiger (b. July 1, 1770, d. January 14, 1841) was the son of John and Ann Murph Geiger. He was married to Dorothy Kinsler. He served as a major in the War of 1812, and was Lexington's first member of the House of Representatives from 1808 to 1815. He also served on the Commission of Free Schools in 1811, the year the Public Free School Act became law.

These first schools were established for the benefit of the state's poor. "Old field schools" provided an adequate education prior to the Civil War. Of those who enlisted in Confederate service, less than 10 percent were unable to read and write. At the beginning of the war, about twenty thousand students were enrolled in free schools.

In 1868, the free school system collapsed and was replaced by a corrupt and inferior Reconstruction school system. Hugh S. Thompson is credited with bringing the school system out of this postwar confusion by establishing a county board of examiners to ensure teacher qualification and a uniform textbook system.

Halfway Ground and School

For traders, farmers and travelers, the Halfway Grounds was a welcome sight. It provided water, repairs and a resting place along the well-traveled road between Zion Church, the ferry crossing; and Granby (replaced Saxe Gotha), the trading post and point where boats could be taken to the Lowcountry with goods to trade. When travelers reached the pond, they knew they were halfway between Zion Crossing and Granby.

In the beginning, the resting place was only a pond along the old Native American trail linking the Cherokee Nations with the coast. Later, Europeans who settled in the area used the Halfway Ground (off Leaphart Road) for the same purposes. There was a blacksmith shop and a cooper located at the stop to repair farmers' broken barrels as their oxen pulled them along the rolling road to market.

Richard Hampton, great-uncle of General Wade Hampton, owned the Halfway Ground prior to the arrival of settlers who began purchasing the fertile land to farm. Sometime around 1800, Mount Hebron Methodist Church was begun, and Martin Hook had a store. By 1833, the small settlement had a school. George Hook was the school's first teacher, with thirteen pupils.

In 1916, the State Department of Education reported that the Halfway School of district thirty-two had grown to three teachers, with 105 students, and the school was in session for 150 days a year. The district's annual revenue was $4,712.65. A new school was built using $3,201.25 of 1916's revenue.

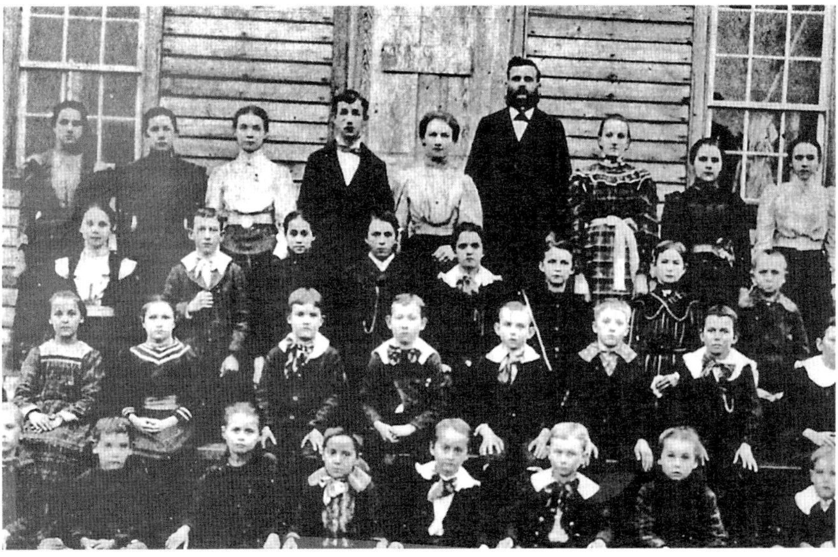

The Halfway School was located between Lexington and Brookland on Leaphart Road.

One Midway School After Another

After a seventy-year absence, Midway School has returned to our community. Long before the present organization of Lexington's five school districts, Midway School was the seat of education for the children of our community.

Minutes from the Young People's Home and Foreign Missionary Society of Ford Road School House of January 8, 1893, show Midway School as a two-story wooden structure believed to have been built near the site of the current Midway School.

The current Midway School is the third school bearing the name of Midway. The second school was a two-room school off Oliver Metz Road. It served the first seven grades, with first through fourth in one room and fifth through seventh in the other. Eighth graders attended high school in Lexington.

Midway students either walked to school or arrived in the family's Model-T Ford. A potbellied wood stove warmed the classrooms while the students read from *Sims' History of South Carolina*, *The Child's World Reader* and *Baby Ray*.

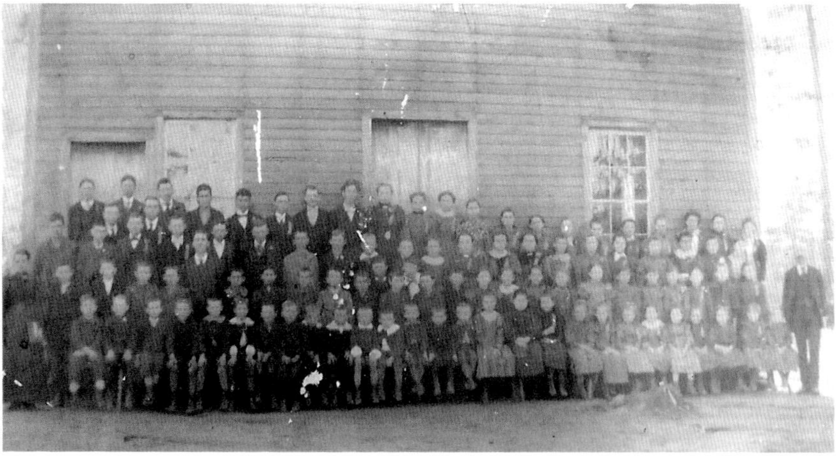

Midway School was located near the Twelve Mile Creek in the Midway community.

The school served other community needs. Before Pilgrim Lutheran Church was organized in September 1899, church services were held at Midway School. When school was not in session, Zion and Pilgrim Churches' parishioners attended special singing schools at Midway, and the school stage was used for performances, plays and community events.

When school districts were consolidated sometime around 1928, Midway School closed. Elementary students began attending school in Lexington, and the Women's League auctioned school items to buy the first cross for Pilgrim Church.

Today's Midway Elementary School is still closely linked with Pilgrim Church. The property for the school was bought from Pilgrim and Martin Meetze, and many of Midway's students attend Pilgrim Church.

Lexington's Lutheran Seminary

It was apparent early in the 1800s that a Southern theology school was needed. Hartwick in New York and Gettysburg in Pennsylvania were the two Northern seminaries. Other denominations were also beginning to establish seats of formal learning to provide a supply of clergymen closer to home.

The Reverend John Bachman of St. John's in Charleston was one of the first to recognize this pressing need for local seminaries. At this point in history, church leaders were beginning to question whether a formally educated ministry was necessary. Reverend Bachman's persuasive arguments prevailed, and in 1829, the South Carolina Synod passed without dissent a resolution establishing a theological preparatory school for boys over the age of ten. The school was to be called the Classical and Theological Institute of the South Carolina Lutheran Synod.

The following year, the board of directors—Godfrey Dreher, John Bachman, William Strobel, Stephen Mealy, C.F. Bergman, West Caughman, John Eigleberger, Henry Horlbeck, Henry Muller and Major Sywgert—raised enough money to begin construction, and in February 1831 the seminary was ready for its first students at the home of Colonel John Eigleberger, in

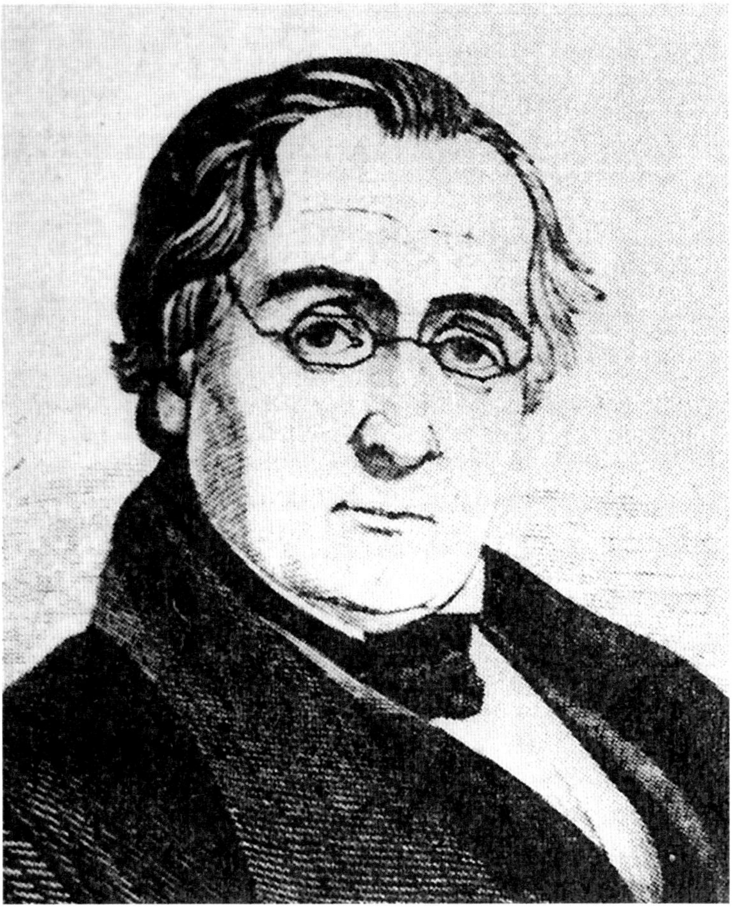

Dr. Ernest Hazelius ran the Classical Academy and Theological Institute in Lexington.

Countsville, Newberry District. The Reverend John G. Schwartz was selected as the school's first professor of theology.

Unfortunately, Reverend Schwartz died a few months later, and a debate arose over the school's location. In a selection by sealed bids, Godfrey Dreher won Lexington as the next site for the fledgling seminary, where it remained for the next twenty-five years.

The Reverend Dr. E.L. Hazelius replaced Reverend Schwartz as head of the seminary. Dr. Hazelius was born in Prussia and was educated in the Moravian Church. He previously taught Latin, Greek and Hebrew at Nazareth Hall in Pennsylvania, but left the Moravian Church when it refused to sanction his marriage, at which time he joined the Lutheran Church. Hazelius also taught at Hartwick and at Gettysburg.

By 1834, the seminary had nine young students, and its first students graduated in 1836. Those first graduates were Frederick Harris, Edwin Bolles, Levi Bedenbaugh, David Bernhard, Henry Stoudemyer, William Berly, Philip Strobel and Elijah Hawkins.

The Classical Academy and Theological Seminary of the South Carolina Synod operated in Lexington from 1834 to 1855. Dr. Hazelius died in 1853, and with him went much of the enthusiasm of the academy. The decline of the school paralleled his failing health.

Newberry College

When the synod met in 1855, it voted to move the school to Newberry. On December 20, 1856, Newberry College was incorporated. A slate of officers was elected, with John Bachman as president; Simeon Fair, vice-president; Henry Summer, secretary; and J.P. Kinard, treasurer.

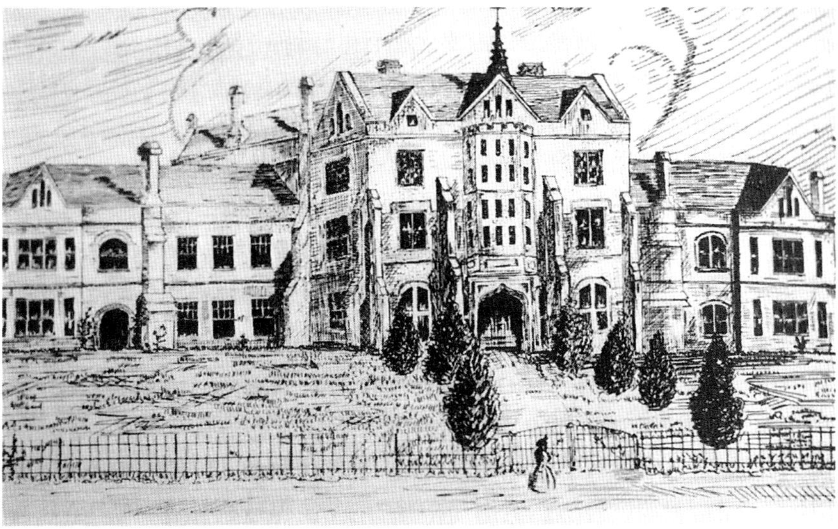

When the seminary closed in Lexington, it moved to Newberry College. The Lutheran Seminary is now located in Columbia.

The task of building soon began. Columbia architect George E. Walker drew up the plans, and the contract was awarded to Newberry builders Wallace Cline and Osborne Wells with a bid of $18,000.

The college opened with 40 students for the summer term of 1858, using only the completed wing of the building. Reverend Theophilus Stork was the college's president. Within a year's time, enrollment had increased to 150 students.

A tuition of twenty-five dollars per session was charged to attend collegiate courses; twenty dollars for classical studies; sixteen dollars for preparatory studies; and twelve dollars for primary classes. Dr. Stork, Robert Garlington, Dr. O.B. Mayer, Dr. John Bachman, Reverend J.A. Brown, Charles A. Stork, Reverend M. Whittle and A.P. Pifer taught courses.

The year 1860 brought the threat of war to South Carolina. Reverend J.A. Brown, then president of Newberry College, left the state for Pennsylvania, and the board elected Reverend J.P. Smetzer of Virginia as its new president. An outbreak of smallpox in May 1860 suspended classes, but the college remained open throughout 1863 and 1864 with reduced enrollment because many of the students had joined in the war effort.

In 1865, as Sherman approached Columbia, the Confederate Army Purveying Establishment moved to Newberry, using the college as its headquarters. At the army's surrender, Federal troops occupied the building. By the fall of 1865, the building was in ruins, with books, furnishings, doors and window shades destroyed or carried off.

In October 1866, the college reopened and eventually was moved to Walhalla for a short time. The college returned to Newberry in 1877, and classes began in the restored college in February 1878.

Possum and Gilbert Hollows

A tale of two cities, twin cities, begins at the junction of two ancient trails—one leading from the Congaree River toward Augusta and the Creek Nation beyond the Savannah River Valley, and the other from the Cherokee Nation foothills and Ninety Six District to Charleston.

And there was the ridge, that great elevation and geographical divide of near mythical proportions. At this point, the villages of Possum Hollow and

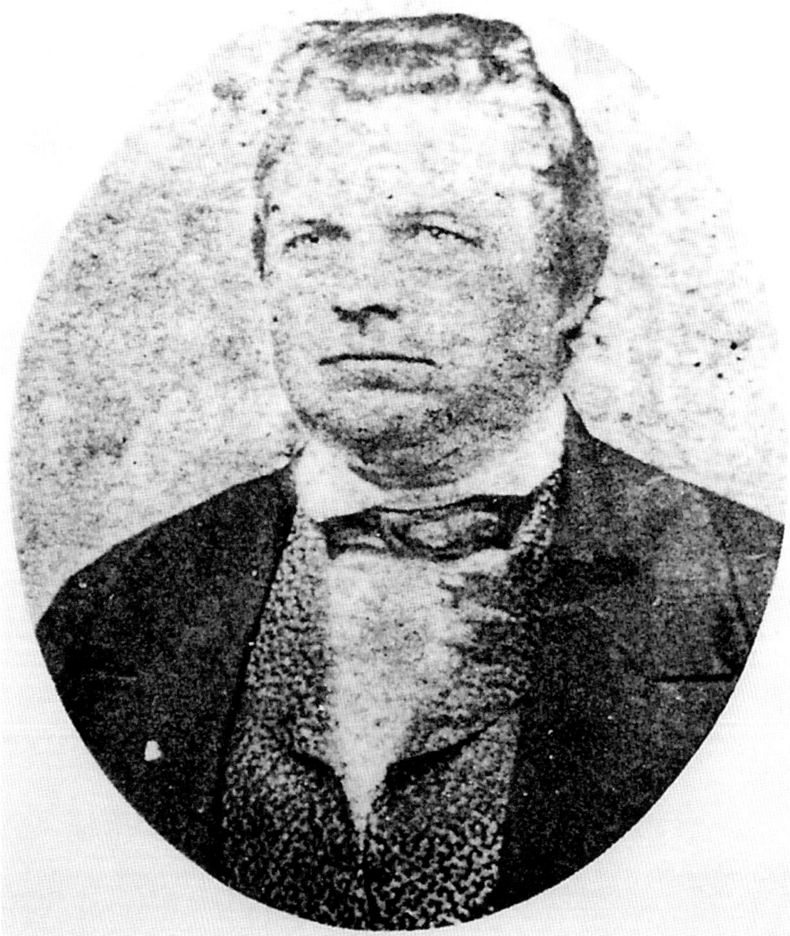

Joseph Andrew Lloyd Lee, descendant of Leesville's namesake.

Gilbert Hollow sprang onto the Lexington landscape with their backs to each other—their cultures, their religions, their people similar, yet different. Possum Hollow faced west toward the Savannah River and Gilbert Hollow faced east toward the Sandhills.

Before either town was begun, the lands had been granted to John Fairchild and Frederick Williams. Fairchild was justice of the peace for Orangeburg Precinct in 1775. He also served in the South Carolina Assembly and was a justice of the quorum. Possum Hollow was organized on Fairchild's lands, and Gilbert Hollow was built on Williams's lands. As the villages grew, they changed their names to Batesburg in 1875 and Leesville in 1877, respectively.

Batesburg was closely associated with the Baptist and Methodist religions, while Leesville was predominantly Lutheran. The renowned Baptist missionary, the Reverend Dr. John Lake, served as minister for the Baptist church near Leesville College.

Leesville was named for John W. Lee, whose family was of English descent. The Lee family purchased land from the Williams family. John's father and mother, Andrew and Nancy Willson Lee, operated Lee's Tavern, a stagecoach stop. It was a resting place for George Washington on his 1791 tour.

Batesburg is the namesake of Andrew David Bates. His family came to the area from the Dutch Fork and Newberry County. Andrew Bates's grandfather, Michael Bates, was one of its first settlers. He was married to Catherine Dreher, daughter of Godfrey Dreher. Andrew was the son of Andrew Dreher and Nancy Ann Shuler Bates.

In the late 1800s, Batesburg-Leesville experienced a surge of new growth as a result of the railroad and excellent educational facilities in the cities. Families and businesses poured into the area. The climate was pleasant year-round, and the location was convenient to the entire state. Batesburg is also the home of former South Carolina Governor George Bell Timmerman, who is now deceased.

Summerland College for Women

Gray Rock Springs was a favorite picnic spot near Leesville, South Carolina. J. William Mitchell owned the spot and built an inn for summer vacationers. He also used the cool, pure spring water for Gray Rock Ginger Ale, which he bottled and sold.

Between 1870 and 1880, Leesville was the home of one of the region's largest and most well-known schools, the Leesville English and Classical Institute, which instructed over one hundred students from five surrounding states. Eventually the school and inn merged into another institution, Summerland Women's College.

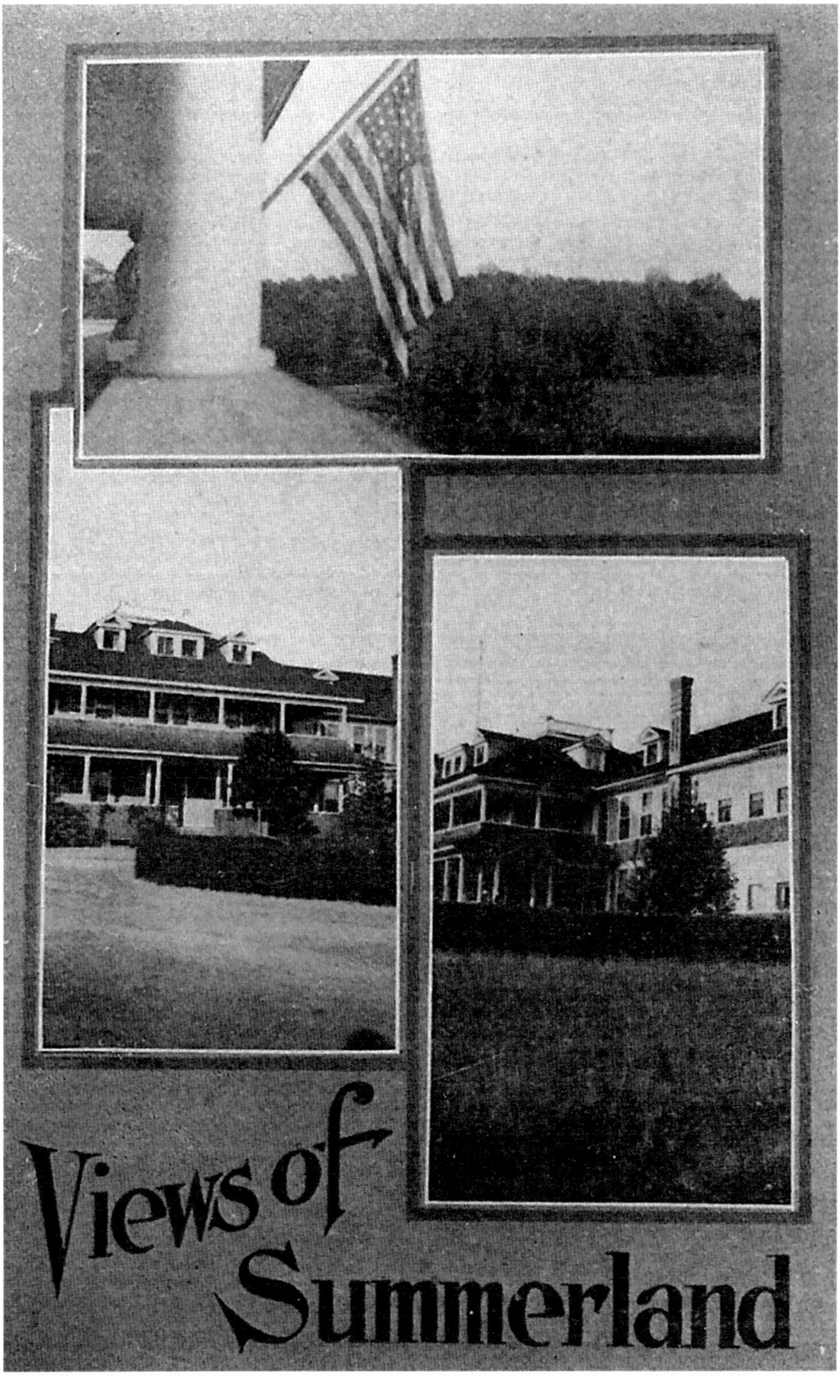

Summerland College in Leesville was a prestigious college for young women.

In 1913, the Summerland Inn was offered to the Lutheran Synod for the purpose of educating young women. The idea was not easy to sell when W.P. Timmerman, W.K. Shealy and L.A. Riser first approached the synod with the proposal, for a variety of reasons. The committee argued that the synod could not support two colleges—Newberry College and a female college. Eventually, with the Lexington vote carrying a majority of twenty-five to twenty-one, the Lutheran Synod accepted the proposal that allowed the synod to have a clear title to the property after twenty-five years use as a women's college.

The project had the synod's vote, but not its financial support. The young ladies had to raise their own funds, which they did very well throughout the years. In fact, the school so prospered that it soon was in need of new and larger accommodations. These were begun in 1920 and opened for students in the 1922 school session.

The Depression years brought on financial hardships for Newberry College. The two schools merged their fundraising efforts, and Summerland's students were accepted as day students.

PART V
Seeking the Kingdom

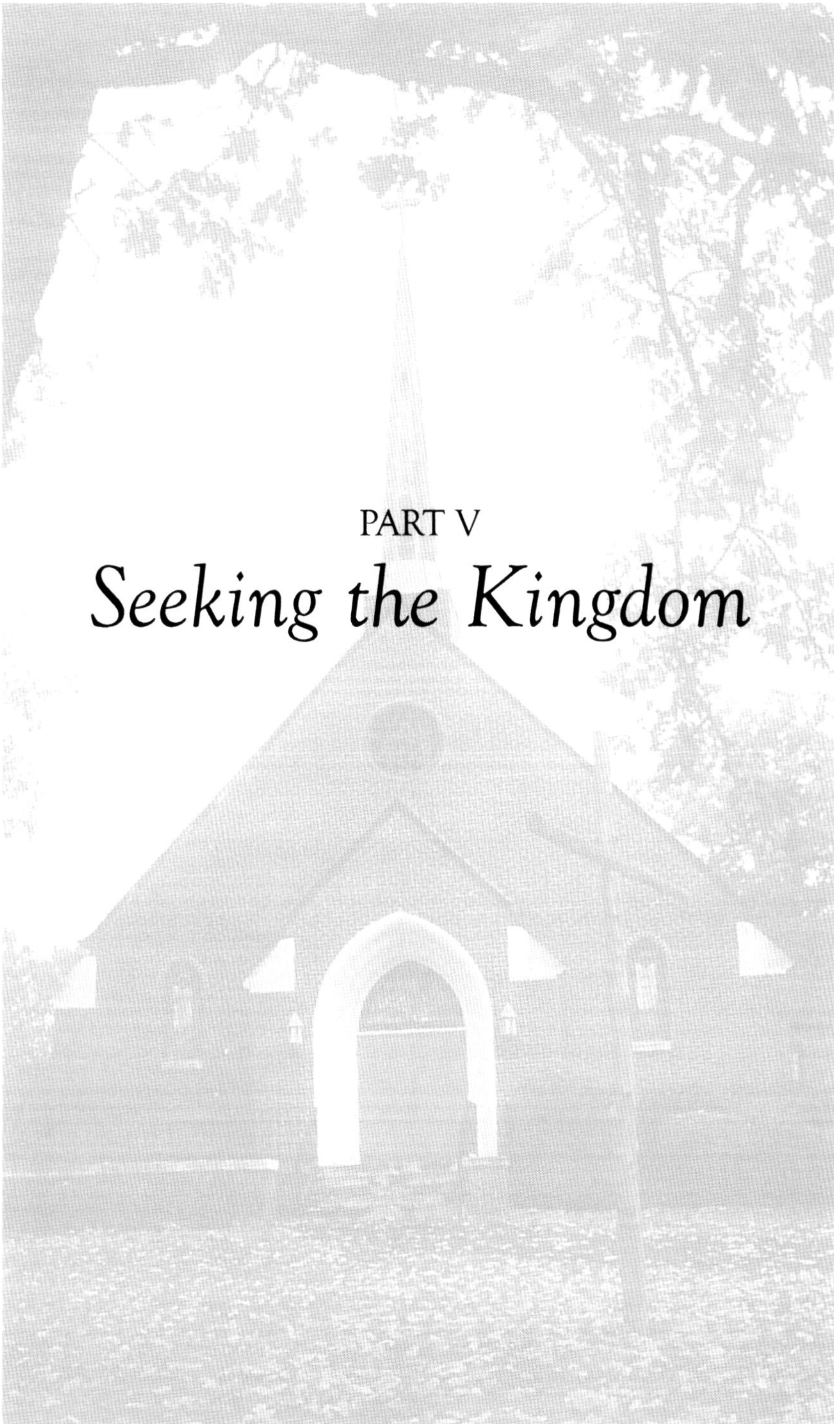

Hessian Mercenary Becomes a Minister

The Reverend John Yost Metz was born in Hesse Cassel on December 2, 1757. As a youth, he was taken from his home during the night by a squad of German soldiers who sold him as a mercenary in America.

As early as 1526, Ulrich Zwingli's argument against conscription became a driving force in the Swiss Reformation. The practice often pitted countryman against countryman on the foreign battlefield. Such was the case with Yost Metz. His forced mercenary service brought him to fight against fellow Germans in South Carolina in the American Revolutionary War. It is believed that as many as seventeen thousand soldiers were enlisted in this manner.

Metz deserted the British army during the siege of Charleston at Bacon's Bridge. He joined with General Nathanael Greene's forces, which brought him to Granby in what is now the Cayce area of Lexington County. It was General Greene who enlisted the services of local heroine Emily Geiger to deliver a message to General Sumter in his efforts to rout General Rawdon from Granby in June 1781.

After the war, Metz was ordained as a Lutheran minister and was instrumental in the organization of the South Carolina Lutheran Synod in 1824. He served Bethel White Rock, Zion, St. Paul's Pomaria and St. Peter's Lutheran Church.

Metz was also a farmer, and he made coach whips and split-bottom chairs. In 1823, near the end of his life, he brought his nephew John Snyder to live in South Carolina from his former homeland. Yost and Anna Gross Metz, themselves, raised a large family.

St. Peter's Church near Lexington, along with Zion and Bethel, are the churches most closely tied to Yost Metz. These three churches formed the Saluda pastorate as early as 1767. In 1780, Metz was minister of St. Peter's near the Eighteen Mile Creek, some four miles from Lexington Courthouse. Services were delivered in both English and German languages.

Metz died May 7, 1833. He is buried near Lake Murray and his beloved St. Peter's Church.

Zion Church of Switzers' Neck

Zion Church was founded between 1740 and 1750 in the Switzers' Neck along the Saluda River at Twelve Mile Creek. The church was incorporated in 1788. John Dreher donated the land for this church near the river.

Prior to 1788, Zion, St. Peter's and Bethel High Hill were part of the Saluda pastorate. In 1787, the same year as the drafting of the American Constitution, German Lutheran and Reformed congregations in the backcountry gathered at Zion to form the Corpus Evangelicum.

In 1792, a church was built closer to the ferry crossing, replacing the first church that had begun as a brush arbor church. In 1856, an addition was made to this structure. In 1922, Zion was moved up the hill to its current location on what was then the Columbia Road. Land for this church was donated by the Corley and Areheart families.

On November 12, 1797, Zion's congregation petitioned the South Carolina Assembly to open a ferry crossing on the Saluda River for the convenience of

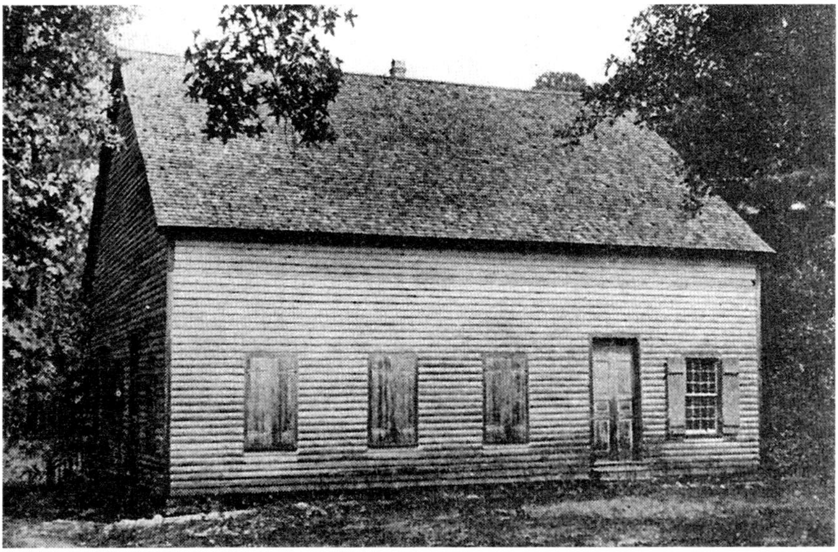

Zion Lutheran Church is one of Lexington County's first churches. It is located on Corley Mill Road.

the parishioners living on the northern side of the river. The congregation also petitioned for support for a minister and a schoolmaster.

Zion's parishioners spoke both English and German, more than likely Switzerdeutsch, a low form of the German language. Many believed German was the language of God and English that of the devil. They preferred to hear their sermons in German, but eventually abandoned German when English became the prevailing language.

St. John's, Pomaria

St. John's, Pomaria, was one of the first, if not the very first, Reformed church in the Dutch Fork. Swiss and German settlers with the familiar names of Epting, Chapman, Summer, Mayer, Haltiwanger, Shumpert and Pressler, led

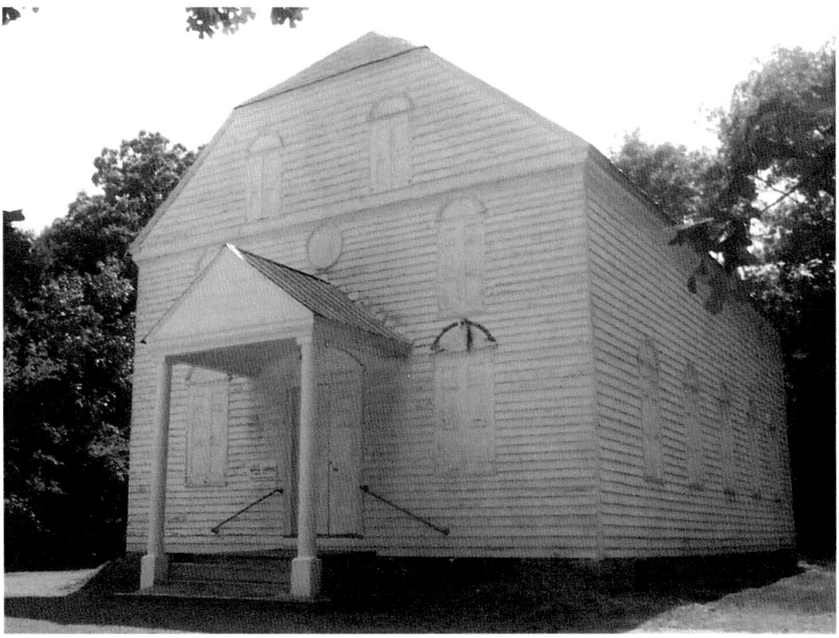

St. John's Lutheran Church (the white church) is also one of Lexington's oldest churches in the Dutch Fork.

by minister John Gasser, formed the congregation that gathered on the banks of Crim's (Grame's) Creek between the waters of the Saluda and Broad Rivers.

St. John's Church was first incorporated in 1763, but the congregation probably organized about ten years prior to this date on lands issued under grant of King George II. St. John's was part of the Corpus Evangelicum of 1788 and was initially called the German Calvinistic Church of St. John's in the Fork. Sometime before 1826, the church became Lutheran under the name Protestant Lutheran St. John Church. This change paralleled the phasing out of the German language in the Dutch Fork.

John Gasser of Turgau, Switzerland, after serving as chaplain in a Swiss regiment, arrived at Philadelphia in 1749 aboard the ship *Elliott.* He did not arrive in Carolina until late 1752. A few years later, he returned to Holland and Switzerland, soliciting support for schoolmasters and books for his congregations in the colonies.

While in Switzerland, he was nearly arrested for attempting to lure Swiss citizens out of the country into Carolina. By this time, Switzerland was ready to stop the flow of emigrants because of the severe labor shortage that had been created by the loss of its people leaving for Carolina.

Gasser must have been somewhat successful in obtaining support from Holland for securing books and a schoolmaster because, according to O.B. Mayer, St. John's was the first schoolhouse built by the German-speaking settlers in the Dutch Fork. Many fine scholars were educated in church school, including Mayer's parents.

In 1809, a new St. John's white church was built with nails and hinges made by John Summer, a founding settler of the Dutch Fork, replacing the old log church. With the new church, the old German school and German language usage declined. After 1826, English was the predominant language spoken in the Dutch Fork, and the old Reformed churches for the most part became Lutheran.

Bethel Church, High Hill

Bethel Church, High Hill, was founded by German-speaking settlers near High Hill Creek and Pender Ridge, Orangeburg District, in 1762. This first church was made of logs, a construction that was typical of frontier churches

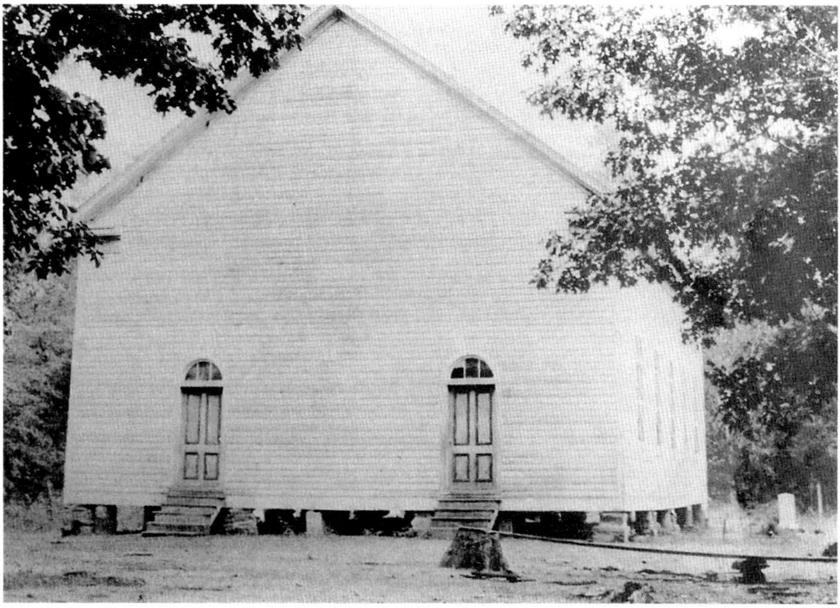

Bethel Lutheran Church, High Hill, in the Dutch Fork.

of the Dutch Fork. John Nicholas Martin of Zwiebrucken, Bavaria, was Bethel Church's first minister from 1767 to 1774. He also served Zion in Switzers' Neck; St. John's, Pomaria; and was most likely the first Lutheran minister in South Carolina's backcountry.

Martin first arrived in South Carolina between 1755 and 1760, and after serving in the Dutch Fork, he became pastor at St. John's Lutheran Church in Charles Town. After the British occupation of Charles Town during the Revolutionary War, the Reverend Martin was driven from its pulpit by British Loyalists who were offended by his refusal to offer prayer for King George. A company of German fusiliers was also raised for the American cause, with a large portion of its members coming from St. John's congregation, further angering Loyalists and forcing the Reverend Martin to leave Charles Town for the remainder of the war. The Reverend John Bachman said of Charles Town's feisty Germans, "During the stormy season of the Revolution the Germans of this city had been strenuous advocates and defenders of the rights of their adopted country."

In 1788, Bethel Church became part of the Corpus Evangelicum along with fifteen other German churches in South Carolina. On January 9 of that year, the Reverend Frederick A. Wallberg, Bethel's minister, signed the unifying petition. In 1810, the congregation joined the North Carolina Synod, and in 1814 a segment of its members joined with St. Michael's Church to use English in its worship services, while Bethel continued its use of German. Bethel was the only church in the Dutch Fork not to join the Tennessee Synod. Bethel later formed a pastorate with Mount Vernon and Mount Olivet in 1894.

The construction of Lake Murray brought further changes for Bethel's congregation. It was learned that the church would be lost to rising lake waters, so Bethel merged its congregation with that of Mount Vernon, and land for a new church building was bought from the Lowman Home at White Rock in 1929, with the new name of Bethel Evangelical Lutheran Church.

St. Peter's, Piney Woods

The history of St. Peter's, Piney Woods Church began on a nine-mile trek of parishioners on their way to attend church services at St. John's in Pomaria. Peter Shumpert noted that a 112-acre tract much closer to their homes than St. John's was unclaimed. So, for the sake of convenience, the land was successfully granted in May 1794 to the congregation, and St. Peter's Church was begun in the thick grove of longleaf pines, giving it the name of Piney Woods. Today, you can find the church on the road leading to Dreher Island State Park near Chapin.

The Reverend Joseph Walleran helped organize the group and served as pastor until 1804. The first church made of hewn logs with pews of split logs and peg legs served the congregation for over forty years. Inside walls and ceiling were made of planed pine boards. When a new church was built, the old structure was sold to Thomas Frick. Some of the old wallboards remain in the family.

In 1834, a new two-story frame church was built that had three doors—one for men, one for women and one for slaves, who sat in the gallery. This church served until 1925, when the current brick church was constructed. Major renovations were made to this building in 1967.

In the early days, St. Peter's produced seven ministers: George E. Long, M.Q. Boland, J.S. Wessinger, V.L. Fulmer, J. Milton Frick, Heyward Epting and John D. Lindler. Early pastors who served St. Peter's were: Godfrey Dreher, Michael Rauch, Daniel Efird and J.K. Efird. Some of the founding families

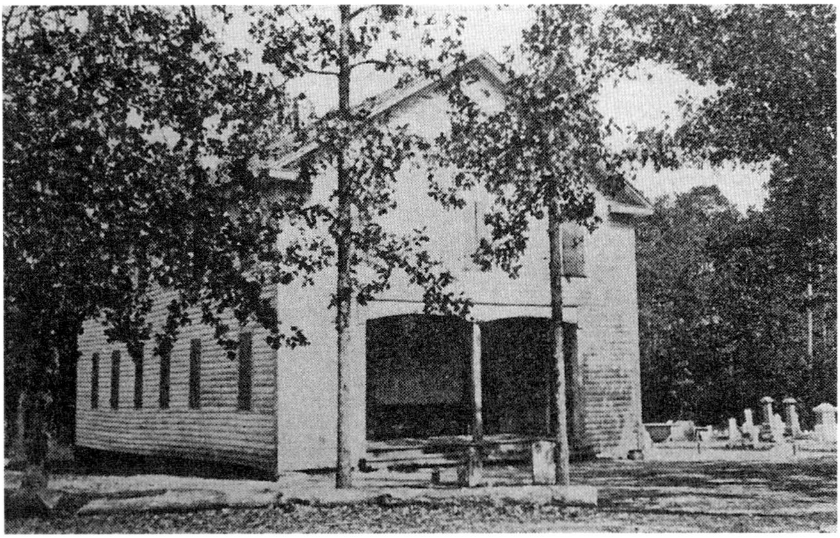

St. Peter's Lutheran Church, Piney Woods, is located in the Dutch Fork.

were the Mayers, Wheelers, Shumperts, Harmons, Seases, Bowers, Wessingers and Fricks.

St. Peter's, Piney Woods, was one of the congregations that remained loyal to Godfrey Dreher in the Dreher Controversy of 1841. In 1842, St. Peter's became a part of the Tennessee Synod, followed by the North Carolina Synod in 1921. In 1922, it became a member of the South Carolina Synod.

Macedonia Celebrates 150 Years

Macedonia Lutheran Church celebrated its 150th anniversary in 1997. Although the earliest church records date from 1905 to 1908, there is much additional information to be found in synod records and recorded historical sketches.

Before 1847, Macedonia's congregation met for public religious services in the nearby schoolhouse. The Reverend George Haltiwanger Sr. served

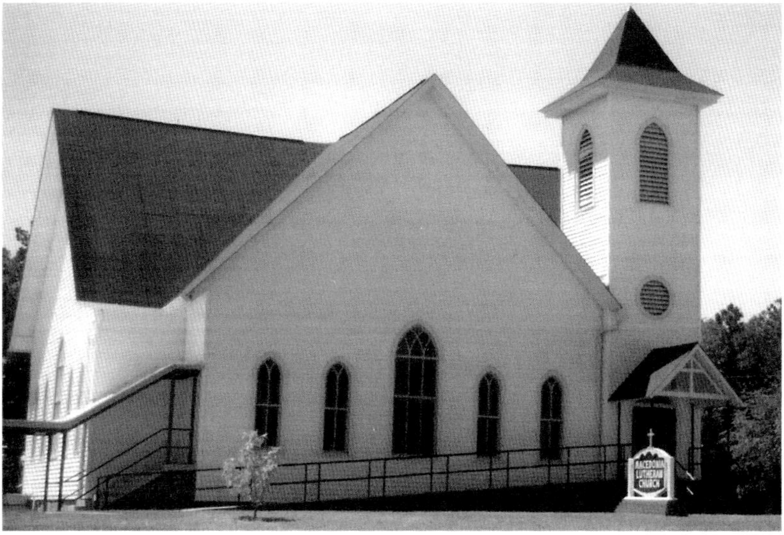

Macedonia Lutheran Church in the Dutch Fork was moved when Lake Murray was built.

as minister once a month. In 1848, the congregation appointed a building committee, and the first church was completed and dedicated in September 1849 by the Reverend William Berley. Some of the oldest members of this congregation bore the names of Dreher, Derrick, Shealy, Epting, Long, Ballentine, Amick and Sultan. There were twenty-three charter members. Many of these members came to Macedonia from St. Peter's, Piney Woods, and St. James (Lybrand's).

Macedonia Church is located in the Dutch Fork of Lexington County on the north side of the Saluda River near St. Michael's Blue Church. It is near the fork of River Road and Caulk's Ferry Road, which crossed the Saluda at Amick's Ferry. (Amick's Ferry was abandoned when Lake Murray was built.) The church sits on a point surrounded by the lake on three sides. Many of Macedonia's founding families were forced to leave their homes and farms, and the congregation was reduced by about one-third.

St. James (Lybrand's) Church was located five miles from Macedonia, north of the Saluda River and west of Bear Creek in Saluda County. Lybrand's was built of hand-hewn logs, twenty by forty feet, and had a goblet-shaped pulpit. Reverend George Haltiwanger also served as this congregation's minister. Lybrand's, St. John's, Zion and other early churches in the Fork and Switzers' Neck share characteristics of the very early Reformed churches.

There was also a commonality among many of the early families. Herman Sultan, an early member of the congregation, like Yost Metz of nearby St. Peter's Church, was a Hessian soldier who came to America during the Revolution. It is believed that the name Sultan was assumed to avoid arrest by the English for desertion. Herman Sultan was the father of Michael, who gave land to Macedonia for its first church.

Salem and Cedar Grove Churches

On March 8, 1792, Andrew and Christopher Kaughman conveyed sixteen acres of land to Salem Church. Records reveal that the congregation applied for membership into the South Carolina Lutheran Synod in 1824, with Reverend Godfrey Dreher as its minister.

Like other early churches in the area, Salem began as a log church. During its 133-year history, three church buildings served its congregations. Salem also served as one of the early schoolhouse churches. Some of the Salem–Cedar Grove members were: Reverend Daniel Efird, Daniel Drafts, David Addy, William Long, Frederick Sease, Uriah Crout, Henry Oxner, Michael Shealy, Jacob Vansant, Adam Risinger and others.

In 1850, a great revival was sweeping the countryside that led to a split in Salem's congregation. The dissenting congregation renamed itself Cedar Grove Evangelical. The two churches shared the Salem meetinghouse for four years, while Cedar Grove prepared to build its own church.

In 1853, Cedar Grove Church joined the Tennessee Synod and remained with this synod for the next sixty-five years, after which time it became a member of the North Carolina Synod. Eventually, South Carolina's Lutheran congregations decided to become one synodical body, and in 1922, Cedar Grove joined with the others to transfer its membership into the South Carolina Synod.

In 1925, a stroke of bad luck hit Salem Church. On the first Sunday morning in December of that year, Salem Church burned down during church services. Pastor W.D. Wise had just begun his lesson for the day. As he read from 1 Peter 4:18—"And if the righteous scarcely be saved, where shall the ungodly and sinner appear?"—the stove flue fell to the floor and fire engulfed the building. There was no water to douse the flames, so all the congregation could do was remove the pews, organ, pulpit and other church furnishings.

With this calamity, the congregation decided to disband—the majority going over to Cedar Grove. A monument was erected to the sons and daughters of Salem Church with the proceeds from the sale of the church's furnishings. Salem deeded its land to the South Carolina Synod.

Salem Church left a fine legacy as the mother church of Cedar Grove and St. Mark's, a church established for Salem's newly freed salves after the Civil War on lands donated by their former owners.

Cloud's Creek Dunkers

> *Send Augusta ministers to New Windsor in hopes to put a stop to the problem of those Baptist vagrants, who continuously endeavor to subvert all order, and make the minds of the people giddy with that which neither they nor their teachers understand.*
>
> —*Lieutenant Governor Bull,* 1770

It is easy to imagine the public outcry that would follow such a statement if it were made today. Attitudes and institutions have changed a great deal in the years since South Carolina was a royal colony. Governor Bull could have been referring to the settlers of Saxe Gotha and Amelia, since many of the settlers in Saxe Gotha and New Windsor were related either by blood, belief or country of origin. One of these early Baptist sects made its way into the northwestern portion of Saxe Gotha, near the Saluda River at Cloud's Creek, and formed the Cloud's Creek Church.

The Reverend John Langford (1728–1796) was listed as an early member of Cloud's Creek Church. At one time he was its minister, but he was no longer preaching in 1791. The Langford family and many of their neighbors moved into South Carolina and Georgia after the battle of Alamance (North Carolina) in 1771. John Langford first settled at Campbell Town near Augusta and New Windsor, but came to Hollow Creek sometime later. Some of the other settlers in the area were the Vansants, Calks, Presnells, Corleys, Kirklands, DeLoachs, Padgetts and others.

Henry Laurens, in his journeys through the Carolina backcountry between 1774 and 1776, made the following observations:

> *On our way we met three carts and one wagon from North Carolina, emigrating to the Oconee lands in Georgia. They consisted of upwards of thirty persons. At about twenty-four miles from Little Saluda we halted at Muddy Springs branch; at twelve more miles crossed a creek with rocky side and bottom, and in six more arrived at Congaree near Friday's Ferry about forty-two miles from L. Saluda.*

As early as 1778, the early Dunkers were organizing in the Cloud's Creek region. The Reverend David Martin served a congregation of thirty families with twelve baptized communicants. This early backcountry church had no meetinghouse and cannot be directly connected with the regular Baptist Church that later organized in the region.

In 1802, the church at Cloud's Creek was officially incorporated, with the Reverend Martin as its minister. Reverend Martin was also instrumental in the Edisto region in organizing Dunker churches, Seventh Day Baptists and a church that would later become known as Healing Springs Church.

Old Lexington Baptist Church

Settlers began arriving in the northwestern region of Lexington about 1750. They came from Virginia and North Carolina, looking for a permanent home.

Without benefit of building or minister, these settlers began their worship of God under the protective shelter of brush arbors. The Old Lexington Baptist Church began in this manner at a place called Gum Spring's Camp on the lands of Asa Langford, grandson of John Langford, early minister of Cloud's Creek Church, later known as West Creek Baptist Church.

Camp meetings were held at Gum Spring until the early 1800s. The farming community gathered at the spring in the lay-by season, late July and early August, for as long as three weeks or more. Entire families would come to the spring in wagons, bringing with them the family milk cow.

The brush arbor was built over the spring and baptismal pool, but services were held under the far-spreading white oaks. This campsite is now under the waters of Lake Murray, near the site of the old Climax School and Daniel Harmon's millpond.

In 1813, the church was officially reorganized, and the Reverend Joseph King was called as its pastor. The first church, located near Lewie's Ferry (later Amick's) and Caulk Road, was a log building that was used for nearly thirty years.

Luther Rice of Northboro, Massachusetts, renowned Baptist missionary, often visited the congregation in its early years. It is thought that his last sermon was given there. He became ill while visiting Pine Pleasant in Edgefield District and died on September 25, 1836. Rice was the first American missionary to Burma and India.

The old church was moved to Saxe Gotha, adding room for slaves, in 1852. One of these slaves, Charity Langford, was a member until her death in 1912. She could neither read nor write, but faithfully quoted scripture. Charity and a number of other slaves are buried in the churchyard.

The church, which is the oldest Baptist church in the area, went by the name Lexington Baptist until another Baptist church was organized at Lexington Courthouse and it became known as Old Lexington Baptist Church.

The Dreher/Moser Conflict

The 1834 South Carolina Synod annual meeting met under a cloud of controversy created by the Reverend Godfrey Dreher (1789–1875) and the Reverend Jacob Moser (1795–1865). The controversy was all about the power of the synod over its ministers and congregations. On one hand, the power was merely advisory; and on the other hand, the synod had the natural right to use power with care "when the minister shall become guilty of a crime or immoral conduct." This ill-defined amendment to the synod constitution eventually instigated the infamous Dreher controversy.

The influence of the early church was giving way to a new generation of leaders. With Martin Boltzius and Christian Theus long dead, and Yost Metz and John Franklow very old men, the young ministers were left with the task of guiding the synod through the development of its constitution.

The controversy began as friction between Dreher and Moser in the fall of 1833. Moser had proposed to lead St. Jacob's Church in a revival meeting, a proposition to which Dreher opposed on the grounds of departure from Lutheranism, and he charged Moser with "acts of gross immorality." Dreher held sermons at St. Jacob's in an attempt to lead the congregation back to the Augsburg Confessions.

Resenting Dreher's intrusion, Moser countered Dreher's charges with his own charges of "preaching certain heretical and dangerous doctrines," publicly aimed at Dreher during one of his (Dreher's) sermons at St. Jacob's. As a result of these actions, both Dreher and Moser were censured and called on by the synod to end their relationship with St. Jacob's.

The next year, Dreher again called on the synod to try Moser, but the synod refused. Dreher then sought intervention by the North Carolina Synod. This resulted in the formation of a committee headed by the Reverend Hazelius to meet with Dreher, but they were unable to resolve their differences. In November, the parties agreed that Dreher should leave the synod on friendly terms and declared Dreher "no longer a minister of our church." The congregations of Zion, St. John's and Bethlehem remained loyal to Dreher and were issued a similar statement—to be "out of the pale of the Lutheran Church."

In 1838, a special conference was held at St. Matthews, Orangeburg District, to deal with church organization and administration. This convention was partially successful in dealing with these conflicting issues and defined church jurisdiction as "purely Spiritual and should not be enforced by the arm of civil power." Five years later, the synod had to once again deal with the issue of Ebenezer's lingering influence (Ebenezer, Georgia, was home to Jerusalem Lutheran Church and the Salzberger colony; the Salzberger ministers were educated in Halle, Germany) by adopting the resolution:

> *In order to remove prejudices, the Synod guarantees to the congregation of Jerusalem, Ebenezer, Georgia, that by the adoption of the Synod Rules and Discipline, their chartered privilege and property, or prospect of future property, are neither infringed nor endangered.*

This final act appears to have resolved the conflict and galvanized the South Carolina Synod's direction.

The Old Blue Church

In 1814, German was still spoken in much of the community, especially among the Swiss. The old German and Swiss first-generation settlers preferred their sermons in the language of the old country.

In time, younger congregations wanted to hear their sermons in English, the language of the fledging country. Many of this younger generation began to break away from older congregations and form new churches that delivered the scriptures in English. St. Michael's Lutheran Church, the Old Blue Church just north of the Saluda River, was one of these churches.

Like its sister church Zion, St. Michael's was organized in a one-room schoolhouse and was part of the North Carolina Synod. The Reverend Godfrey Dreher was its first minister, with the Reverend J. Yost Metz serving as co-minister. The Reverend Dreher is buried in St. Michael's churchyard.

Many of St. Michael's founding members came from Bethel Church at High Hill, where sermons were delivered in German by the Reverend Franklow and in English by the Reverend Dreher.

In 1824, the South Carolina Lutheran Synod was organized at St. Michael's Church by the Reverends John P. Franklow, J. Yost Metz, Godfrey Dreher, Michael Rauch, Jacob Moser and Samuel Herscher. Godfrey Dreher was elected first president of the synod. Samuel Herscher was its fist secretary.

In 1850, the old schoolhouse was torn down to make way for a new building on land donated by John Dreher. This second church was built in the Reformed style and boasted a blue ceiling. The Blue Church came from this—a name that the church retains to this day. A third, the present church on River Road, was built in 1919.

Providence Church

Organized in 1866, Providence Lutheran Church, located off Old Chapin Road, is a scion of Zion and St. John's Lutheran Churches. The church began with sixty-five members under the ministry of the Reverend J.N. Derrick. Reverend

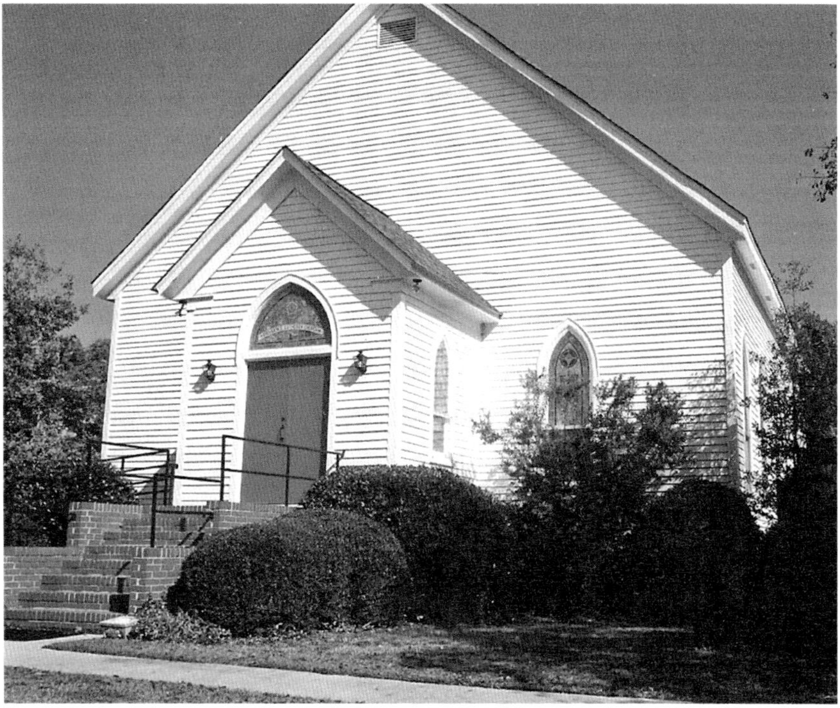

Providence Lutheran Church, Lexington, near Fourteen Mile Creek.

Derrick also served St. Michael's, Bethel-White Rock and St. John's and eventually moved on to Georgia and Mississippi, where he died in 1894.

Many of Providence's members relocated when Lake Murray was built. A son of Providence's congregation, George Baylis Corley, who married Barbara Ruth Dennis of Summerville, was an exceptional seminary graduate. He was ordained in 1949 at the age of twenty-five and served churches in Ehrhardt, Georgetown, Newberry and Cameron. He was also business manager of the *South Carolina Lutheran* magazine.

Many of the people who organized Providence belong to Lexington's old families—the Roberts, Wingards, Corleys, Rauchs and Cooks. George Baylis Wingard and his wife Lucy Cook Wingard, daughter of Julia Roberts and William Cook, are buried in Providence's churchyard. While Lucy Baylis, as she was known, attended Providence, George Baylis attended St. John's, where he served as Sunday school superintendent for forty years.

Lucy Baylis was noted throughout the community for growing huge pink tomatoes from seeds she grew and collected for over twenty years. At age eighty, her sewing skills won her first place in the Lexington Dress Review, and at age eighty-five she won first prize at the state fair for her quilt. Her husband, Baylis Wingard, was a noted farmer in his own right. In 1915, he was recognized as champion peanut grower of the world.

The Wingards enjoyed the friendship of the whole community, and for many years friends and relations of the Wingard family celebrated the Fourth of July at Wingard Springs as guests of Lucy and George Baylis Wingard.

St. John's, Lexington

Whether you travel by boat or car, you are likely to hear the bells of St. John's Lutheran Church on the old Caulks Ferry Road along Lake Murray's western shoreline.

St. John's serves as a landmark for German settlement along the Saluda River between Lexington and Hollow Creek. The German Protestant Church was established in 1832 by Godfrey Dreher and Michael Rauch. In 1835, the Lutheran synod approved the congregation's petition, and sometime prior to 1847 the church was renamed St. John's Lutheran Church.

St. John's first church was built on a three-acre lot purchased from Jacob Rall for eight dollars. This church was a wooden-frame structure with a slave gallery, built on a model much like many other neighboring Reformed churches. The timbers were hand hewn and nailed together with handmade wooden pegs. In 1956, the wooden church was dismantled and replaced with its current brick church.

St. John's first pastors were Michael Rauch, Godfrey Dreher, George Haltiwanger, J.H. Bailey and A.W. Lindler. Families who made up the first congregation were the Ralls, Harmons, Seases, Rauchs, Hydes, Kellys and Hendrixes.

In the early years, around 1881, St. John's shared a parish with St. Stephen's, Sandy Run and Providence. The following decades brought several changes in parish structure, and in 1969 Providence and St. John's formed a parish.

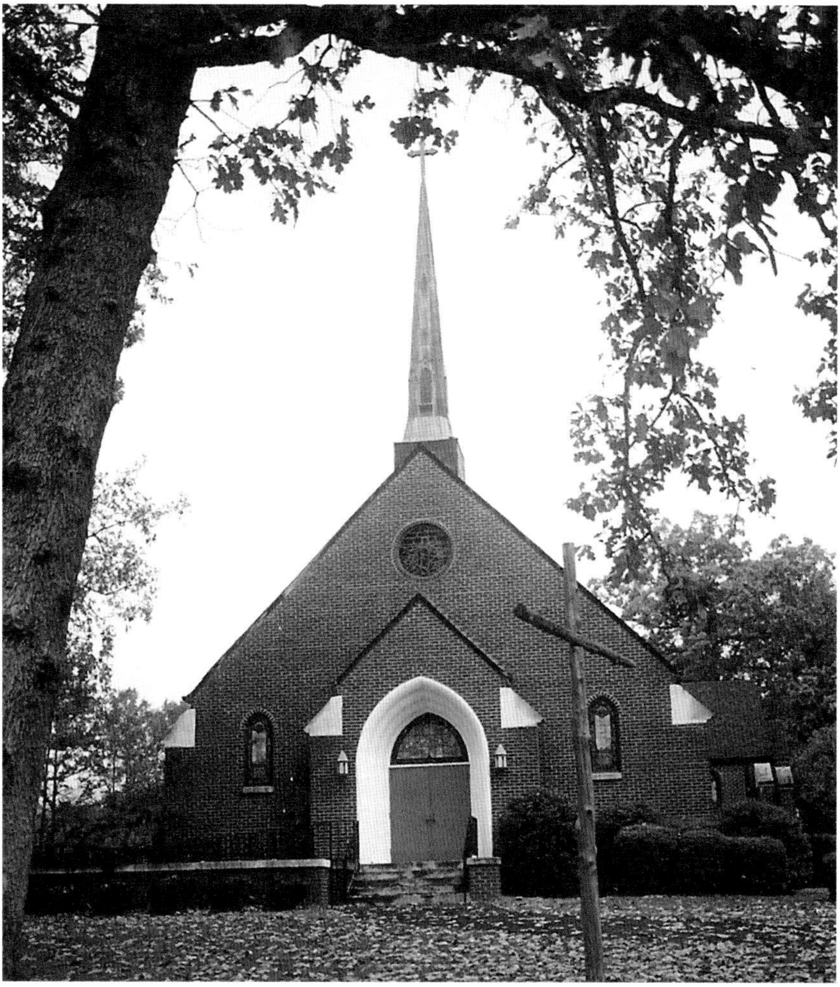

St. John's Lutheran Church, Lexington.

Good Shepherd, Swansea

Marylou Haigler Pushkar, who grew up in Swansea as a member of Good Shepherd Lutheran Church, related the following:

When the men of the church were building the parsonage, they came to mama's house for their noon meal. The weather was so hot, they would take a midday nap in the large hall, taking advantage of its cool linoleum floor.

Ms. Pushkar is now a member of Incarnation Lutheran Church in Columbia, South Carolina.

The Lutherans of Swansea were a minority among the South Lexington community's Baptists and Methodists. It was in April 1912 that the church was organized under the leadership of the Reverend William Bowman Aull. Good Shepherd was built on the corner of Lady Street and Monmouth Avenue in Swansea, on land purchased from John W. Goodwin for $400. There were nine charter members: J.B. Coates, Amanda Coates, Nettie Crapps, Mr. and Mrs. S.J. Derrick, J.M. Gunter, James L. Haigler, Willie Haigler and Joseph Reeder.

Frank Hildebrand made three pieces of chancel furniture for the congregation, and there were two odd chairs, a reed organ and a potbellied stove. Pews were of the slatted, handcrafted variety, and there were no paraments. Members raised money for a piano by performing plays.

In the early years, services were given by a supply minister who came twice a month on Sunday afternoons. In 1915, a women's home and foreign mission was organized by the Reverend D.B. Groseclose. Mrs. J.B. Coates, Sallie Hutto, Mrs. S.J. Derrick, Annie Mae Haigler, Minnie McCullough, Emma Lightsey and Sallie Haigler were members.

The ladies' circles worked tirelessly for the congregation. Over the years they bought pulpit chairs, flower stands and made paraments. They began the mother-daughter banquet, made Chrismon ornaments, hand stitched a Christmas banner and sponsored the Golden Age Dinner honoring the church's older members.

Good Shepherd provided one son to the ministry, the Reverend Alvin Hayne Haigler, son of Thaddeus S. and Mary Gnann Haigler, who was ordained in 1959. He served in Lutheran churches in Lexington, Newberry, Columbia and Sumter.

In 1949, under the leadership of Pastor Joseph Alonzo Shealy, the church began to grow, increasing its membership and starting a building program. As a result, Sunday school classrooms and a parsonage were added. The Reverend Paul Counts was the first to reside in Good Shepherd's new parsonage.

For eighty-six years, Good Shepherd has been a spiritual beacon in the Swansea community, making up in benevolence what it lacked in numbers.

St. David's, West Columbia

St. David's Lutheran Church, West Columbia, was organized in 1840 by the Reverend J.F.W. Leppard with seven charter members. According to Schimer's sketches of early churches, the congregation held services in a brush arbor and the old schoolhouse until 1845, much like Zion and some of the other early county churches. A frame building was eventually constructed, and in 1908 a larger church was built to accommodate its growing congregation.

It would be over one hundred years, in 1956, before St. David's became self-supporting with its own minister. After this time, the congregation grew more rapidly, and by 1962 a contemporary Gothic church was built that could seat six hundred people.

Pastors serving St. David's in its early years were Reverends Leppard, George Haltiwanger, J.B. Lowman, A.D.L. Moser and William Berley. Two sons of the congregation became ministers. They were Daniel Murray Shull and Frank Roof. Reverend Shull was ordained in 1930 and served Zion, St. John's, Bethel-White Rock, Mount Olivet and others. Reverend Roof was ordained in 1935, and served churches in Tennessee, Virginia and Greenwood, South Carolina.

A second-generation member of St. David's, Jesse Marion Roof, had planned to become a minister, and would have if the Civil War hadn't interrupted his studies. Jesse Marion Roof began studying under the Reverend David Shealy of White Rock. Every two weeks he made the ride on horseback to the Reverend Shealy's home to study the catechism. He planned to continue his studies at Lexington Theological Seminary. The war changed those plans, but he never lost his love of the scriptures or his church.

Jesse Marion Roof married Reverend Shealy's daughter Tarzy on January 27, 1859. On April 1, 1861, he enlisted in the Confederate Company H, Twentieth South Carolina Infantry Regiment. Throughout his life, Jesse Marion was a fervent supporter of St. David's Church. He and his wife Tarzy, along with several of their children, are buried in St. David's churchyard. Their home still stands in the St. David's community.

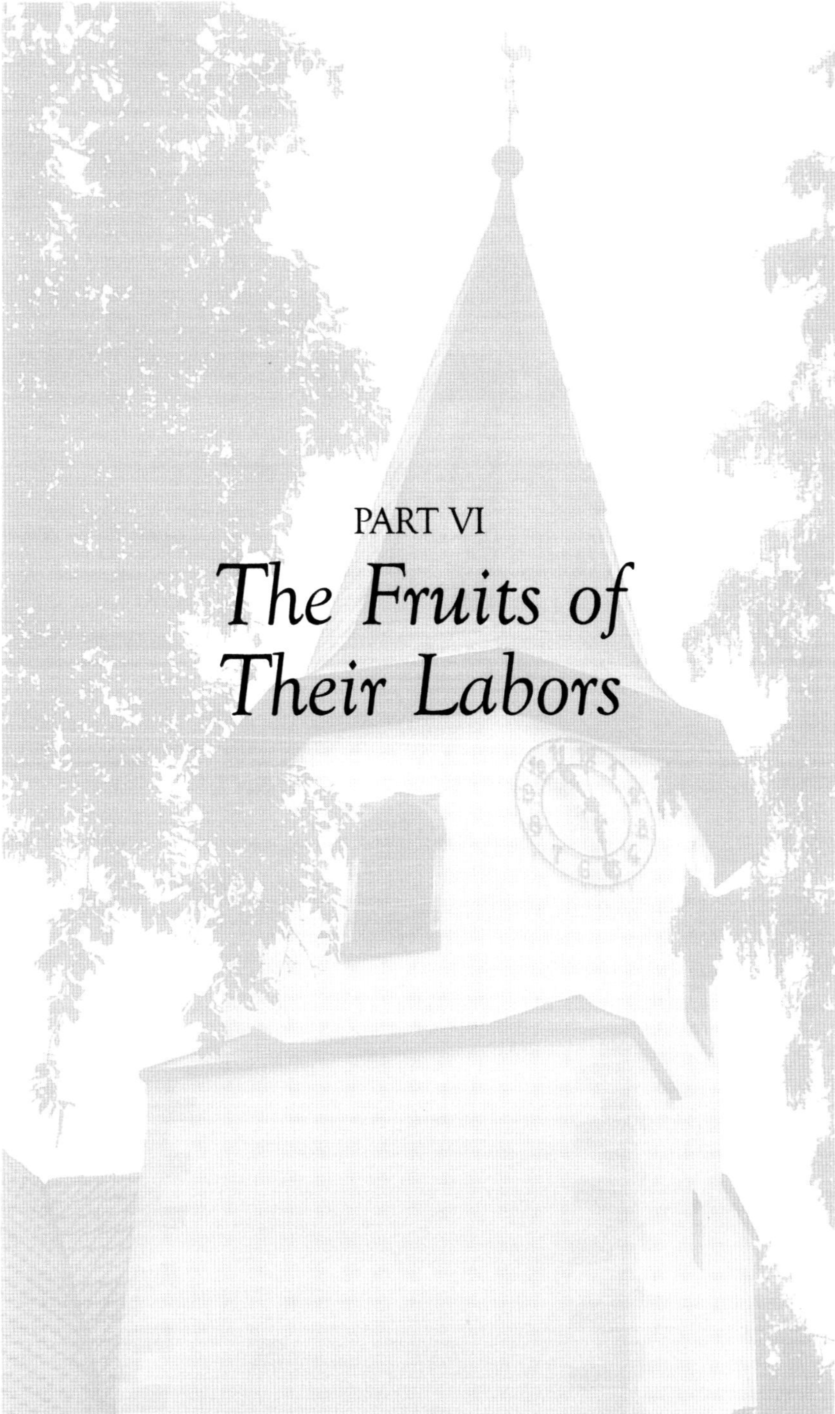

PART VI
The Fruits of Their Labors

The Fridays of Saxe Gotha

Martin Friday (1689–1758) arrived in Charles Town with his wife Maria Magdelana Dysli (m. March 10, 1715) and children Jacob, Anna Maria, Elizabeth and Barbara on July 13, 1735, aboard the *Samuel*. Martin was the youngest son of Peter and Christina Fridig of Fruitegen, Canton Bern, Switzerland.

Martin Friday had read Peter de Pury's pamphlet telling of the wonders and opportunity of Carolina and was persuaded to leave Switzerland to chance a new destiny in the Carolina colony. On March 13, 1735, the Fridig family set out for Rotterdam on the Rhine River from Bern, Switzerland. An account of the journey was published in the *Bermesche Aris-Blatter* on June 4, 1735.

> *After they left here* [Bern] *they were fifty-three days on the way to Rotterdam because of bad weather and water, but contrary to expectations they passed the Rhine safely and without mishap, but with three times as much expense as they had expected and on May 19th they arrived in Rotterdam...The 21st of May 300 of them embarked in one ship.*

Two days later, they arrived at the Isle of Wight. After a brief stay, they departed England in June 1735 aboard the ship *Samuel*, bound for Carolina.

Martin Friday's final destination was the Congarees, later called Saxe Gotha. Many of these early settlers traveled up the Santee River to the falls and Tom Brown's trading post. Friday was eligible to claim 250 acres of land, which he did. His claim was granted on September 16, 1738, in Charles Town.

In the years that followed, at least five more children were born to Martin and Maria. They were John Martin, David, Nicholas, Gabriel and Daniel. With an expanding family, Martin Friday claimed more land. He established a gristmill on Falls Creek, and the family located its home on the main road through the township. The Fridays accommodated many visitors and traders as they traveled through Saxe Gotha.

In 1750, Martin Friday opened a ferry crossing a mile and a half above Fort Congaree at Falls Creek. Sometime around 1755, Friday purchased a second mill on Twelve Mile Creek in the northern section of Saxe Gotha Township. The Fridays were members of Zion's early congregation, and his will lists his household goods at the Twelve Mill Creek location.

Martin Friday's son Gabriel was born in 1752 in Saxe Gotha Township and died in 1830 at the age of seventy-five. His grave can be found behind the Northside Baptist Church in West Columbia on Double Branch Road. He was married to Anna Mary Kinsler, widow of John Kinsler, who was killed by a Tory assassin's bullet. Gabriel Friday inherited one hundred acres of land from his father and the rights to operate the ferry crossing.

During the American Revolution, Gabriel Friday organized and equipped a company of Patriots with his own funds for General Thomas Sumter. Captain Friday served the cause for independence with great courage and was known for his daring. When Lord Rawdon captured Fort Granby, several of the local militia were captured and taken to Charles Town along the Old State Road. Captain Friday enlisted a small band of soldiers and rescued the captives, one of whom was Colonel Thomas Taylor, who was to be tried in Charles Town.

The Tarrer Family of Lexington District

George and Jacob Tarrer sailed from Germany into Philadelphia aboard the *Saint Mark* in 1742. By 1765, the Tarrers were settled in the Dutch Fork of South Carolina. Jacob and Juliana Elizabeth Tarrer and their family received a grant of four hundred acres of land between the Broad and Saluda Rivers in 1768.

Two of Jacob and Juliana's children, Frederick and Andrew, appear in the early records of Zion Church of Switzers' Neck. These children were contemporaries of Abraham Geiger, Godfrey Dreher, Samuel Friday and Laurance Corley. Andrew married Catherine Corley Drafts, widow of Michael Drafts and daughter of Laurance Corley.

It is known that Jacob supplied horses and feed to the Continental army during the American Revolution.

Andrew and Catherine bought 241 acres of land on the Twelve Mile Creek east of the town of Lexington. They built their home at Tarrer Springs, near the rock quarry pond and site of the skirmish of Tarrer Springs during the Revolution. Their home was a stagecoach stop on the old Columbia to Augusta road. Aunt Katie was well-known for her generous hospitality.

Andrew and Catherine had seven children: Nancy, Jacob, Julia, Harriet, James, Frank and Betsy. After Andrew's death in 1840, Catherine and her daughter Betsy ran the stagecoach stop. It is believed that Andrew, Catherine and some of their children were buried in the family cemetery at Tarrer Springs.

Other members of the Tarrer family moved into Columbia and are buried at Elmwood Cemetery. Jesse Tarrer, grandson of Jacob and Juliana, moved to Macon County, Georgia, with his wife and family in 1842. They bought land near Fountainville. Jesse and Miley Hoffman Tarrer took six children with them to Georgia. They were Henry, Joseph, Susannah, Jacob, James and Belinda. John Luther was born after they settled in Georgia. Eldest son Henry migrated to Texas. Jesse and Miley are both buried at Mount Zion Lutheran Church in Macon County.

Daughter Belinda married Jesse Huffman on April 23, 1835, according to Godfrey Dreher's journal. It is believed that the two sons of Belinda and Jesse Huffman later went on to Tupelo, Lee County, Mississippi.

The Kleckleys of Switzers' Neck

Johannes Kleckley came to America in 1750 aboard the ship *Friends, Good Will* with his three sons Gotlieb, Johannes and Ludwig Kleckley (Klack). Johannes was granted two hundred acres in Ninety Six District, which he traded for land in Saxe Gotha. In 1776, he purchased land on the south bank of the Saluda River from John Michael Smithpeter, son of John George Smithpeter, who was murdered by Jacob Weber in 1761.

The Klack family originated in the Wertenburg-Frankfort area of Germany (modern-day Bavaria). The late historian Clayton Kleckley visited Lindau on the northern shore of Lake Constance on the German-Swiss border.

Gotlieb Klack became Godfrey Kleckley in the Switzers' Neck. He and his wife, Nancy Kell, also settled along the banks of the Saluda River. Gotlieb and

Nancy had one daughter, Nancy, who married Dave Wingard. This branch of the family is now in Georgia. Gotlieb married a second time to the daughter of John Oswald. They had four known children: David, Harriette, Susanna and another son who was killed by Native Americans. Gotleib's tombstone records his date of death as February 9, 1819.

Johannes Klack became John Kleckley. Johannes and his wife, Mary Ann Wessinger, settled near the Saluda River. His gravesite is unknown, but many descendants remain in Lexington. One son, John H. Kleckley, was sheriff of Lexington between 1846 and 1852. He also served as county auditor from 1882 until his death in February 1887. John H. built and ran the Kleckley Mills on Twelve Mile Creek. He is buried in a Kleckley family cemetery alongside his brother, Daniel Kleckley, and his wife, Ellen Corley Kleckley, off Oilver Metz Road in the Midway area of the county.

Ludwig became Lewis after moving to Orangeburg, where the family name changed to Cleckley. The Orangeburg Cleckleys of today can trace their ancestry to his two children, Jacob Cleckley and Mary Cleckley Houser.

Early members of the Kleckley family were part of old Zion Church's congregation, and many still remain active in the Zion Church of today.

Father Jacob's Dream

Jacob Kleckley (November 1, 1791–April 23, 1862) was the son of John Kleckley and Catherine Long of Switzers' Neck. He was raised along the Saluda River in the years following the American Revolution. Jacob married Fannie Hamiter (his third wife) and attended Zion Church. They were happy and prosperous.

In time, Jacob heard the ministerial calling to become a Lutheran pastor. He served St. Jacob's on the Wateree Creek and St. Peter's (Meetze's) near Lexington. At the age of forty-eight, in 1839, Jacob heard another call—that of the Georgia wilderness. At the urging of David Coogler, Jacob and Fannie made the long trip to Macon County, Georgia, to establish a Lutheran mission church. On lands secured from J.F. Robinson, Jacob built a meetinghouse at Dutch Level, Georgia.

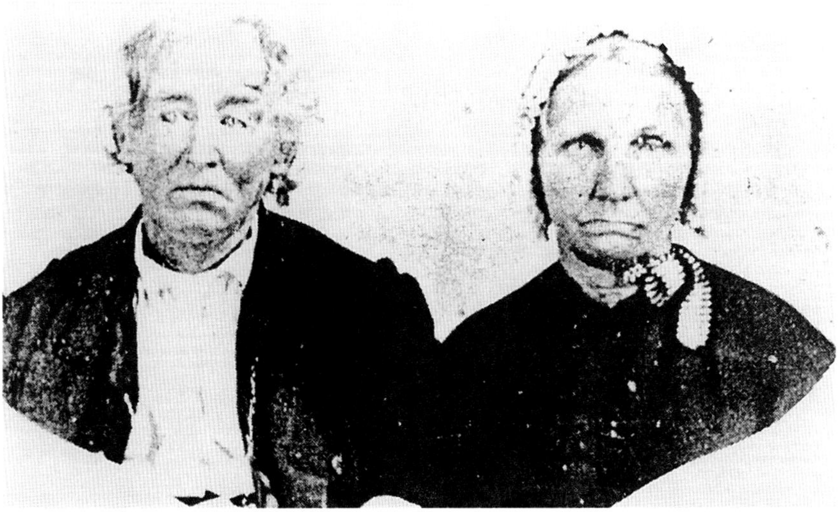

Jacob and Fannie Kleckley moved to Georgia to start a Lutheran church there.

Father Jacob, as he became known, brought more Lutherans from South Carolina to Oglethorpe, Georgia, in 1840. Mount Zion was named for his home church along the Saluda River.

Jacob Kleckley, along with four other Lutheran pastors, founded the Evangelical Lutheran Church of the State of Georgia and Adjacent States in 1860. Throughout the years, until the founding of the Georgia Synod, Father Jacob traveled the 250 miles to South Carolina annually to attend South Carolina's Synod meetings.

Father Jacob and Fannie brought kindness to the Georgia wilderness. They visited the sick, took Georgia's orphaned children into their own home and preached the word of God in the wilderness. Georgia's mission church was Jacob's dream that has endured through two centuries. His missionary spirit can be observed to this day in his descendants, one of whom is Rosalind Carter of Americus, Georgia.

Jacob and Fannie lost three sons in the Civil War. Daniel died at Fort Pulaski, Jacob at Cedar Run, Virginia, and John at Petersburg. Disheartened by the hardships of war, Father Jacob Kleckley died in April 1862. Fannie lived until 1883.

How Many Ways Can You Spell Metz?

The first Metzes to arrive in Saxe Gotha were John Henry Metz, his wife and three children. In 1742, they claimed 250 acres between the Broad and Saluda Rivers. The Metzes (Meetzes, Metts, Metzgers) were German settlers in the Dutch Fork.

John Henry's neighbors were Solomon Ade (Addy) and Martin Hafemejer. In 1766, Christopher Metz arrived aboard the *Britannia* from Amsterdam and claimed three hundred acres on the Edisto River in Amelia Township, Orangeburg District. Christopher Metz's lands bordered those of Henry Felder. Also listed is Joseph Metz, who received eighty acres in Orangeburg District on High Hill Creek.

The will of Henry Metzger of St. George Parish, dated October 10, 1777, reads:

> *I leave to my wife, Margaret, rent from a house on King Street, Charles Town, during her lifetime, and all my lands in said parish. Daughter Margaret, said house at the death of her mother. Executors shall sell land on the fork between Saluda and Broad Rivers next to Isaac Horse, land at Highhill Creek in Amelia Township, and land on the Savannah River; residue of estate to three children.*

According to Margaret's will, dated August 30, 1784, she married a second time to Henry Bysell.

The spelling of these names differs from those of the Dutch Fork and Saxe Gotha, but similarities of land ownership and acquaintance are striking.

Early German records show that Henrich Metz was born in Reinheim, Strakenburg, Hesse, in 1653. His father was Johannes Metz. His mother was Else Jackel Metz, and his maternal grandparents were Matthew and Anna Schneider Jackel.

Yost Metz was the son of John Christopher and Elizabeth Kneibe Mutze of Ederbringhausen, Germany. Yost Metz married Anna Margaret Gross. Their children were John Yost Metz, who married Nancy Caughman; Jacob; Margaret, who married David Hendrix; Nancy, who married James Graham; Elizabeth, who married Wesley Caughman; Rebecca, who married Edwin J. Scott; Catherine, who married Emanuel Corley; Felix, who married Jane Bourne; and Henry, who married Carolina Elizabeth Dreher.

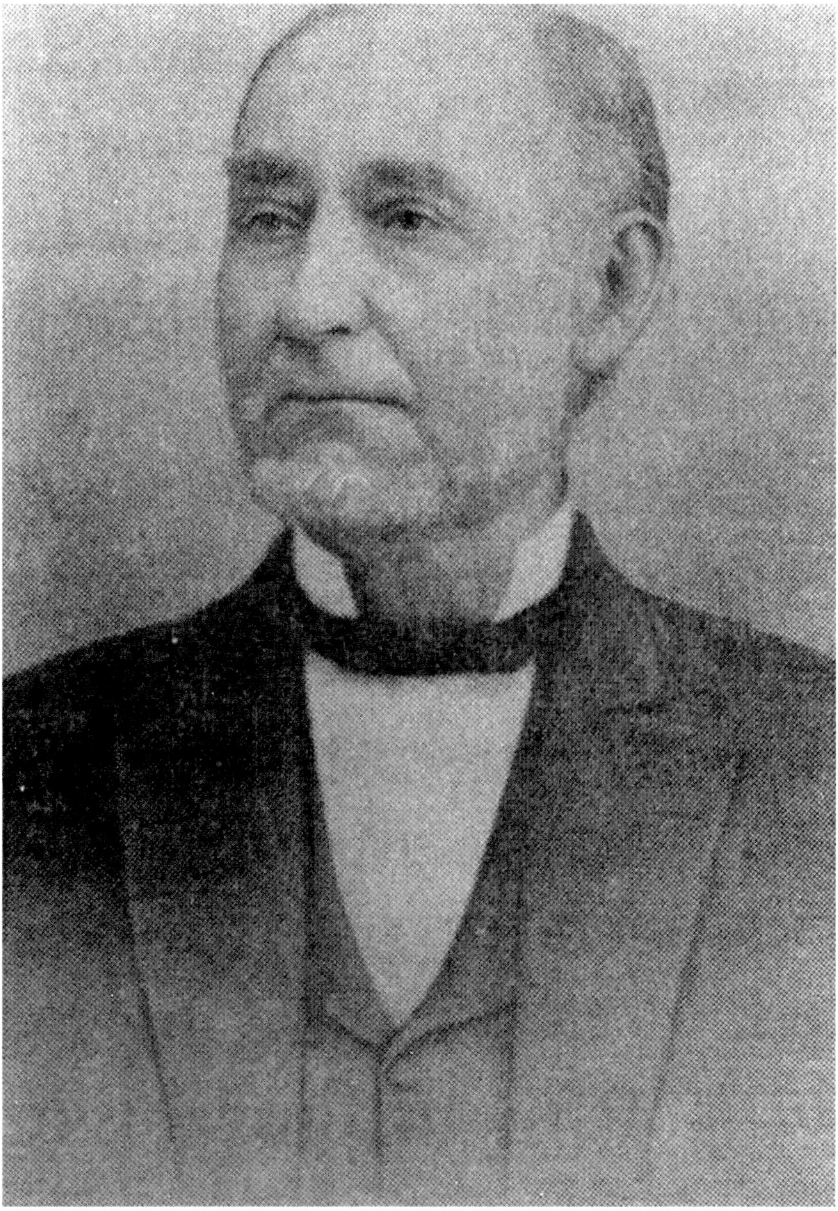

Henry Meetze of Lexington helped save Lexington's court papers when Sherman marched through.

Metz later brought his nephew, John Snyder, to South Carolina in 1832. Snyder was a blacksmith and soldier in the Prussian army that followed Napoleon into France after his defeat.

Good Stewards in the New Land

Another family that settled in the Carolina backcountry was the Wingard family. The first of this family in Carolina was John Adam Wingard, who arrived in Charles Town in December 1752 aboard the ship *Elizabeth* with his wife Anna Barbara and their five children: John Mathias, John George, George Michael, Mary Margaret and Catherine. Another child, Christian, is known to have been born after their arrival in Carolina.

There is record of Hans Wenger, who arrived in Charles Town in 1735 after being blown off course on his way to Pennsylvania. Hans was granted two hundred acres in Carolina, but died shortly after receiving his grant. His wife, son Lazarus and daughter Anne resettled in Pennsylvania under the name of Wingard. Hans Wenger and his family originated in Guggisburg, Canton Bern, Switzerland, but were designated as Palatines in Pennsylvania.

In 1753, John Adam Wingard petitioned the council government for 350 acres of land at Cloud's Creek in Ninety Six District. John Adam arrived at Cloud's Creek shortly after Isaac Cloud and Native Americans massacred his family. And it is believed that John Adam Wingard was killed before January 18, 1760, in these uprisings. Anna Barbara and her children sought shelter at Fort Fairchild on Bear Creek on the north bank of the Saluda River; the fort is now under the waters of Lake Murray. Fort Fairchild was built by Thomas Fairchild and served as a British stronghold during the Native American uprisings of the 1750s, and continued to serve as a source of refuge for backcountry settlers into the 1760s. Tories destroyed the fort during the Revolution.

After the Cherokee uprisings of the 1760s, Anna Barbara acquired lands near Saxe Gotha on the Sixteen Mile Creek at Wingard's Spring. Today, commuters pass through Wingard lands along Pilgrim Church Road, past the old Rikard's Nursing Home and beyond.

The generations of Wingards that followed John Adam and Anna Barbara have served Lexington and its people well. Simon Peter Wingard was one of these descendants, whose home was located on U.S. 1 across from the Lexington County Library. He is credited with saving much of Lexington's court papers when Sherman marched through Lexington by hiding them in the swamp at Bear Creek. Wingard served as clerk of court, sheriff, probate judge and senator.

The Po' House

In days gone by, in a time before social security, Medicare and nursing homes, most of our community's matriarchs and patriarchs were honored heads of their own households—it was a time when folks just took care of folks. Nonetheless, there were elderly and infirm in our community who needed assistance. George Wingard recognized this need and gave ninety-seven acres of land for an almshouse, or as some folks called it, the Po' House.

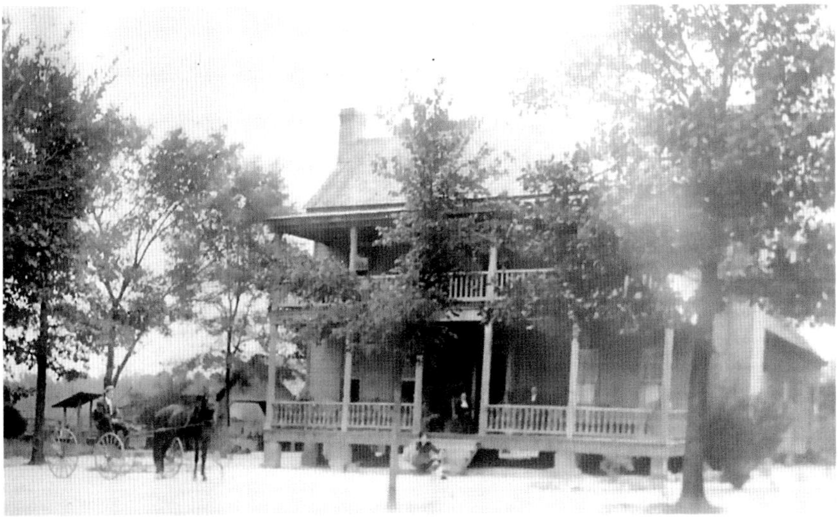

The George Baylis Wingard home, located on Old Cherokee Road in Lexington County.

In 1770, land located at the present site of Lexington Medical Center Extended Care facility was in the Wingard family, settled by George Michael and Anna Maria Oachs Wingard. George Michael and Anna Maria had nine children: George, Michael, Benjamin, Daniel, Gabriel, Samuel, Barbara, Catherine and Thomas Wingard Sr.

George Michael and Anna Maria's eldest son, George (1773–1843), was the donor who made an almshouse possible. George was married to Nancy Hipp, who was the daughter of John Hipp, a prosperous ferryboat operator in Lexington County. George followed his father-in-law into the boat-running business and operated a boat between Peak and Charleston. George and Nancy had four children: George II, Nancy, Millie and Elizabeth. Elizabeth (Mrs. John Swygert) and Millie (Mrs. David Coogler) later immigrated westward with their husbands and lived out their lives in the West.

The Po' House was a well-run establishment. Life was simple and the rooms dark and dreary. The main buildings had eight to ten rooms, with three to four patients to a room. Many of the rooms were windowless, but the porch that ran the length of the building provided fresh air and a place to socialize. Religious services were held once a month by ministers in the community, and in time an organ was purchased for musical accompaniment.

In addition to the living quarters, the home provided a place for burial. There were two cemeteries—one for the patients and a potters' field for condemned criminals when no family member came to claim the body of an executed prisoner. Sheriff Henry Corley was appointed to carry out executions by hanging.

In 1949, the Po' House became Rikard's Nursing Home. At the urging of Mrs. Bertha Rikard, a public welfare worker, the county commissioner granted her authority to open a privately run nursing home, thus allowing patients to become eligible for public assistance and to receive nursing care.

Simon Peter Wingard

In 1829, Samuel and Catherine Bickley Wingard had a son who would play a major role in Lexigton's history. Simon Peter Wingard took some of the sting out of the destruction Sherman had planned for Lexington by saving many of the court's records.

Simon Wingard was clerk of court of the Lexington District Court of General Sessions and Common Pleas. He was discharged from the Confederate army to fulfill the obligations of clerk of court, a position he held until 1868.

Wingard saved court records from Sherman's torch by burying them on his farm near Bear Creek in the Dutch Fork. As expected, Sherman did, indeed, burn the courthouse. When court sessions resumed, they met in the Methodist church on East Main Street until a new frame courthouse could be built at the old site.

Throughout his life, Wingard held various public offices. After his political disabilities were removed in 1872, he served as probate judge for twelve years and was Lexington's state senator from 1884 until 1887. Prior to the war, he was sheriff and commissioner of roads. During the war, he served as a private in the Fourteenth Battalion and Fifth Regiment of the South Carolina Calvary. He was also an elder of St. Peter's and Cedar Grove Lutheran Churches.

Simon Wingard was married to Mary Ann Maria Wingard, daughter of Jacob and Christine Lybrand Wingard. They had seven children: James, Sudella, Mary, Paul, John, Simon Adam and another son who died in infancy.

The family lived a mile below town on the Augusta Highway. The home had an interesting history. It was built in 1850 on the old Jake Drafts place. For a while it was owned by Wilkins Gunter, and at another time by a Mr. Morris from Vermont who made quite a successful attempt at grape culture. The house was moved from its original location across the highway and was demolished in 2005.

Both Morris and Judge Wingard made improvements to the property, which at one time was considered to be the "most comfortable, convenient, and improved home in the county."

Simon Wingard died in June 1909 of heart failure and is buried at St. Stephen's Lutheran Church.

George Baylis Wingard

George Baylis Wingard, born in 1861, was the son of Thomas Adam and Nancy Monts Wingard. He and his wife, Lucy L. Cook Wingard, had seven children: Leola Pearl, Daniel Ira, Jannette Julia, George Shelton, Zula

Elizabeth, Cora Mae and Nancy Luannie. He died in 1926 much as he lived—simply, honorably and among his kinsmen.

George Baylis Wingard was an extraordinary farmer, breaking many growing records. He served in the South Carolina House of Representatives from 1916 to 1918 and was family historian and chairman of the Wingard family reunion.

During World War I, the Lexington community of German and Swiss descendants felt the bitterness of anti-German sentiment, but it was without regret that these descendants took up arms and fought bravely for America. George Baylis Wingard loved South Carolina and Lexington County. He honored his heritage. In a speech he made at the Wingard family reunion after the close of World War I, he offered encouraging, healing words to his kinsmen. He said:

> *South Carolina has taken the lead in many things, and can always be depended upon to be found in the forefront. She built the first railroad in history to be operated by steam. South Carolina has the largest cotton mill in the world, Olympia Mill in Columbia. She holds other records for having produced the largest yields per acre of both cotton and corn.*
>
> *Just as South Carolina is the greatest state in the Union, so is Lexington its greatest county. Lexington has sent out more ministers than any other county in the state. In the last one hundred years, this county, in addition to Methodists, Baptists, and other denominations, has sent out eight Lutheran ministers. She has about forty Lutheran churches besides those of other denominations, and has a larger number of Lutherans than any other county in South Carolina.*

George Baylis Wingard went on to name some of Lexington's leading citizens: Honorable A.F. Lever, who served eighteen years in Congress, was chairman of the Committee on Agriculture of the House of Representatives and was appointed a member of the Federal Farm Loan Board by Woodrow Wilson; Honorable D.J. Griffith, who served as superintendent of the state penitentiary for eighteen years and whose son served as mayor of Columbia; Dr. S.J. Derrick of the Dutch Fork, who served as president of Newberry College; and B.H. Rawl, who was appointed chief of the U.S. Dairy Division and Bureau of Animal Industry.

George Baylis Wingard concluded with a final note of praise for his community:

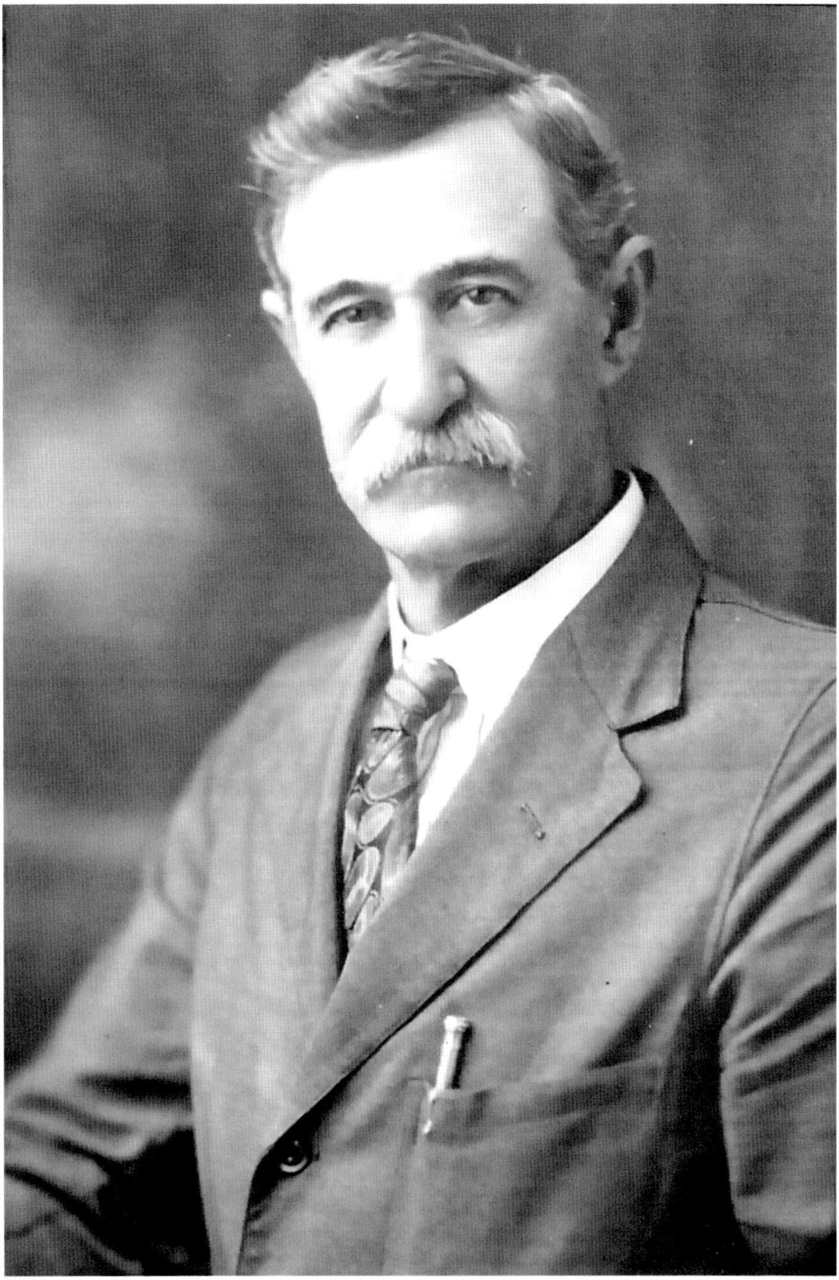

George Baylis Wingard served in the state legislature, representing Lexington County.

Nobody in this community is rich, but nobody is poor, nor is wealth the all important factor in greatness. In this community, practically every person does his own thinking, attends to his own business, and performs his own work. I want to remain here as long as I live, and I want to be buried here on the land that my fore parents chose for their home, and that good old spring [Wingard Springs] *down there is good enough for me.*

A Pilgrim's Journey

In 1752, Johannes Schule, his wife and six children sailed down the Rhine River to Rotterdam and on to the port of Charles Town to begin a new life, free to worship God as they pleased in the Carolina backcountry.

In Unterhausen, a village of about six thousand inhabitants in southern Germany, there is a church, St. John the Baptist Lutheran Church. Unterhausen is located in the valley that rests beneath the once protective realm of Liechtenstein Castle. St. John the Baptist Church is the place where Lexington's Shealy ancestors married, baptized their children and expressed their Protestant faith in the turbulent Reformation years.

The Reverend Hans Felder, a retired Lutheran minister, related the 413-year history of St. John the Baptist Church to the group of thirty-two Shealy travelers who made the trip to Germany in June. Lexington's Shealys were introduced to Unterhausen's Schules with the assistance of a German translator, and for a brief time the lost relatives of another time and place had returned. The two sets of families exchanged gifts, shared meals together and gave accounts of family history since their parting so many years ago. Ten days hardly seemed enough time to catch up on lost centuries.

Nothing was quite as moving or as memorable as the small Lutheran church filled with Alpine flowers welcoming the return of long forgotten kinsmen who had been seemingly lost forever. The natives had returned and, with their return, transcended time. The bridge of kinship and common faith spanned centuries of separation—ten days had become an eternity, two centuries but a moment.

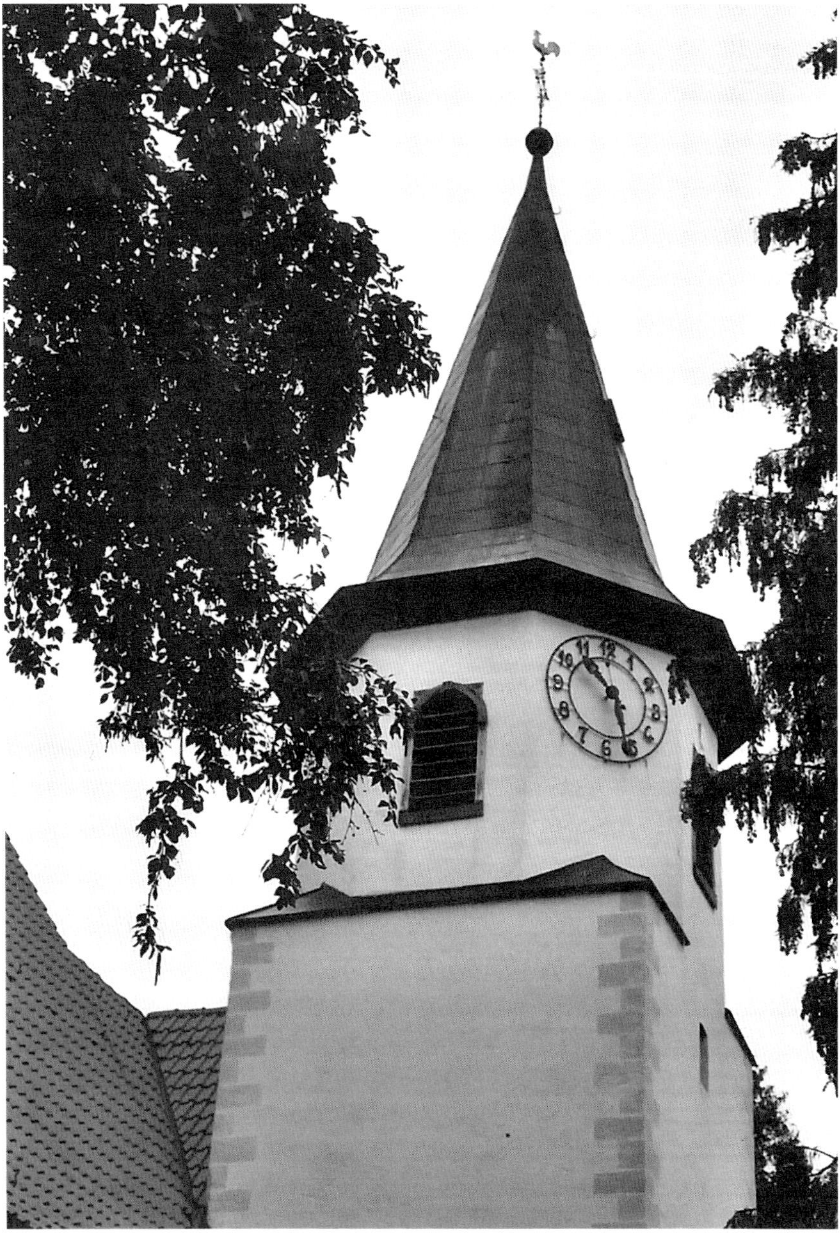

A Reformed church steeple in Bavaria, Germany.

The Quattlebaums

The first Quattlebaums to settle in the Dutch Fork were Johannes, Peter and Mathias. The brothers settled in Carolina's backcountry in 1765. They were the sons of Peter and Barbara von der Hutte Quattlebaum of Kettwig, near Mulheim in the Rehur district of Bavaria in southern Germany. The name "Quattlebaum" means plum tree, and the term "to plant your quattles" means to plant for posterity.

Peter, Barbara and their five children arrived in Philadelphia aboard the brigantine *John of Perth Amboy* on October 19, 1735. Four other children were born in the family after they arrived in Pennsylvania. Quattlebaum family records can be found in Berks and Lehigh Counties, Pennsylvania. Three daughters were married in Philadelphia at St. Michael's and Zion Reformed Church. Gertraud married Carl Huynt on March 7, 1746; Maria Catherine married Jacob Urnstadt on March 3, 1748; and Anna Margaretha married Eberhardt Kunkel on January 3, 1749.

Peter died at age fifty in 1748. He is buried in Kensington, Philadelphia. Youngest daughter, Johanna, died shortly after her father and is buried there

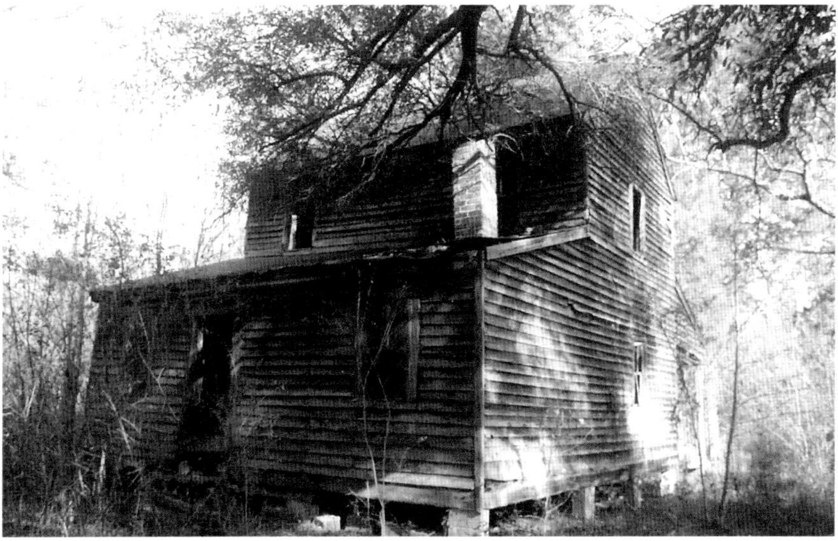

The John Quattlebaum house south of Leesville on Lightwood Creek.

also. Peter's widow and the remaining children moved south into Virginia and eventually to South Carolina.

Mathias Quattlebaum settled on Crim's Creek in the Dutch Fork and established a mill site. He was married to Rachel Derrin. Mathias served under William Houseal in the Revolutionary War, and his mill provided cornmeal and flour to the American troops. Mathias died between 1803 and 1808. Mathias and Rachel's children were Maria Christine, Thomas Shadrack, Mathias, Moses Ezekial, Leah, Rachel, Gertraud and Nancy.

Peter Quattlebaum married Catherine Cappleman, daughter of George and Lovey Cappleman. Their children were Elizabeth, Margaret, David, Peter, Joseph and Sarah.

Johannes first settled along the Saluda River in Saxe Gotha. His first wife apparently died, leaving him with four small children. Census records show that he and his family were living in Edgefield District in 1790. During the Revolutionary War, Johannes served under General Francis Marion and met a Miss McDuffey, whom he later married. It is said that they shared their first meal together on the bottom side of a barrel in the Pee Dee Swamp. Johannes's children were John, George Washington Quattlebaum and two daughters whose names are unknown. Johannes died sometime before 1820.

Quattlebaum's Mill and Rifle Works

Captain John Quattlebaum was born on December 1, 1774, on his father's plantation on Lost Creek in Saxe Gotha. He was raised in Edgefield District. In 1815, after returning from the War of 1812, he came to the Leesville area at Lightwood Creek on Brodie's Pond and ran a cotton gin, gristmill, lumber mill and flour mill and began to manufacture the Quattlebaum rifle.

Captain John was married twice. He was first married to Sarah Weaver and then to Metee Burkett. Later in his life, Captain John's health began to fail and he lost his eyesight. Captain John died on November 28, 1853, at Pinarea, the home of his son Paul.

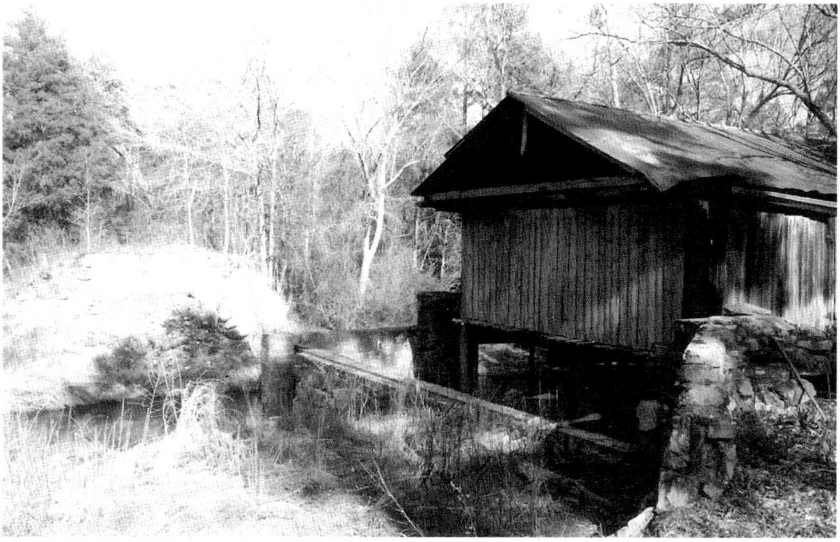

The Quattlebaum Mill was the site of Quattlebaum's Rifle Factory prior to the Civil War.

General Paul Quattlebaum was born July 8, 1812. He grew up at Quattlebaum Mills and distinguished himself through his military and public service. In 1835, the governor requested that he raise a company of volunteers for the Seminole Wars in Florida. His company was part of the First Regiment, Infantry Bull's Brigade, South Carolina Volunteers, that engaged Chief Osceola and nearly captured him at a Florida farmhouse.

Paul was married to Sarah Caroline Jones, daughter of Colonel Mathias and Clara Perry Jones of Ridge. They raised nine children: Paul, Virginia, Claudia, Theodore, Edwin, Olivia, Bolliver, Cephas and Charles.

General Quattlebaum served in the state House of Representatives from 1840 to 1843, and the state senate from 1848 to 1851, representing Lexington District. While serving in the senate, he worked on the committee to construct the statehouse.

General Quattlebaum improved upon the innovation of the family mills, gin and rifle works left to him by his father. He installed what is thought to be the first water-turbine wheel and circular saw used in sawmills in South Carolina. He built a new flour mill, which ran day and night six days a week. Wheat was hauled in from neighboring plantations with six-mule teams and provided flour for much of Columbia and the Confederate army during the war years.

The Quattlebaum Rifle Works thrived under Paul's management. He manufactured what is thought to be South Carolina's first percussion-cap lock mechanism, which he mounted on a barrel of his own design. During the Civil War, the Confederate army leased his rifle works, and all guns produced there went to the army. Eventually, the rifle works was sold and became Hall Rifle Works.

Paul died in 1890 at the age of seventy-eight at his home, Pinarea.

The Ruff and Sox Families

The first Ruffs (Roofs) arrived in the Dutch Fork at Little Mountain, formerly known as Ruff's Mountain, sometime around 1748, having come to Carolina from Pennsylvania. Johannes Sebastian Ruff was the first of his family to claim a hundred-acre land grant. He was originally from Hesse, Germany.

Sebastian had two brothers, George and Daniel, who also settled with him in the Dutch Fork. Sebastian's son, Johannes Melchoir Ruff, also acquired lands on the south side of the Saluda River near the Twelve Mile Creek, 50 acres on Buffalo Creek in Newberry District and 200 acres in Berkeley County. In 1787, he bought an additional 750 acres under the new tax law. Together with his brothers, the Roof-Ruff family owned much of the land between Oak Grove and the Saluda River.

Sebastian was one of the founding elders of Zion Church along the Saluda. He and John supplied provisions for the Continental army. John Ruff was married to Catherine Cromer, whose family came from Baden, Germany. They had thirteen children.

Daniel David Roof was John and Catherine's thirteenth child. He married Nancy Amanda Sox, daughter of Gottlieb and Katherine Gross Sox. Gottlieb was the son of Henrich Sachs of Germany, who arrived in Charles Town Harbor in 1744 with about three hundred other passengers who had been stripped of their clothes. The group had encountered pirates in the Atlantic who saw fit to relieve them of their valuables and clothing.

The settlers stayed offshore until hemp sacks could be provided to cover them. Henrich died in Charleston around 1790. Gottlieb brought his mother and the rest of the family to Lexington, where he purchased lands.

Gottlieb and Katherine Sox built a large home at the Sycamores, a

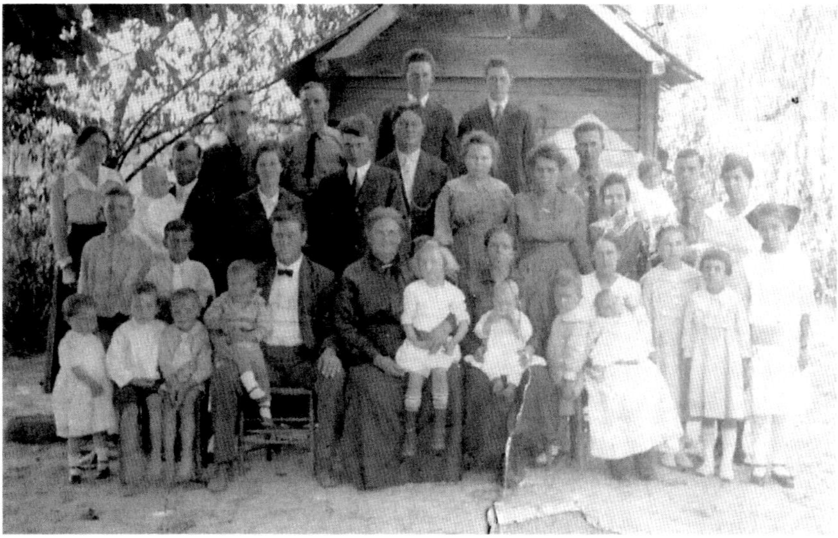

The John Gehardt Mathias Sox family of Edmund are descendants of Lexington County's founding families.

stagecoach stop on Highway 1 between Columbia and Lexington. This is the spot where George Washington stopped when his horse went lame, causing him to layover in Columbia an extra day.

The Roof and Sox families, both early members of Zion Church, were instrumental in establishing Emanuel Lutheran Church around 1850 and Mount Herman Lutheran Church in 1910.

PART VII

Above All, Endure

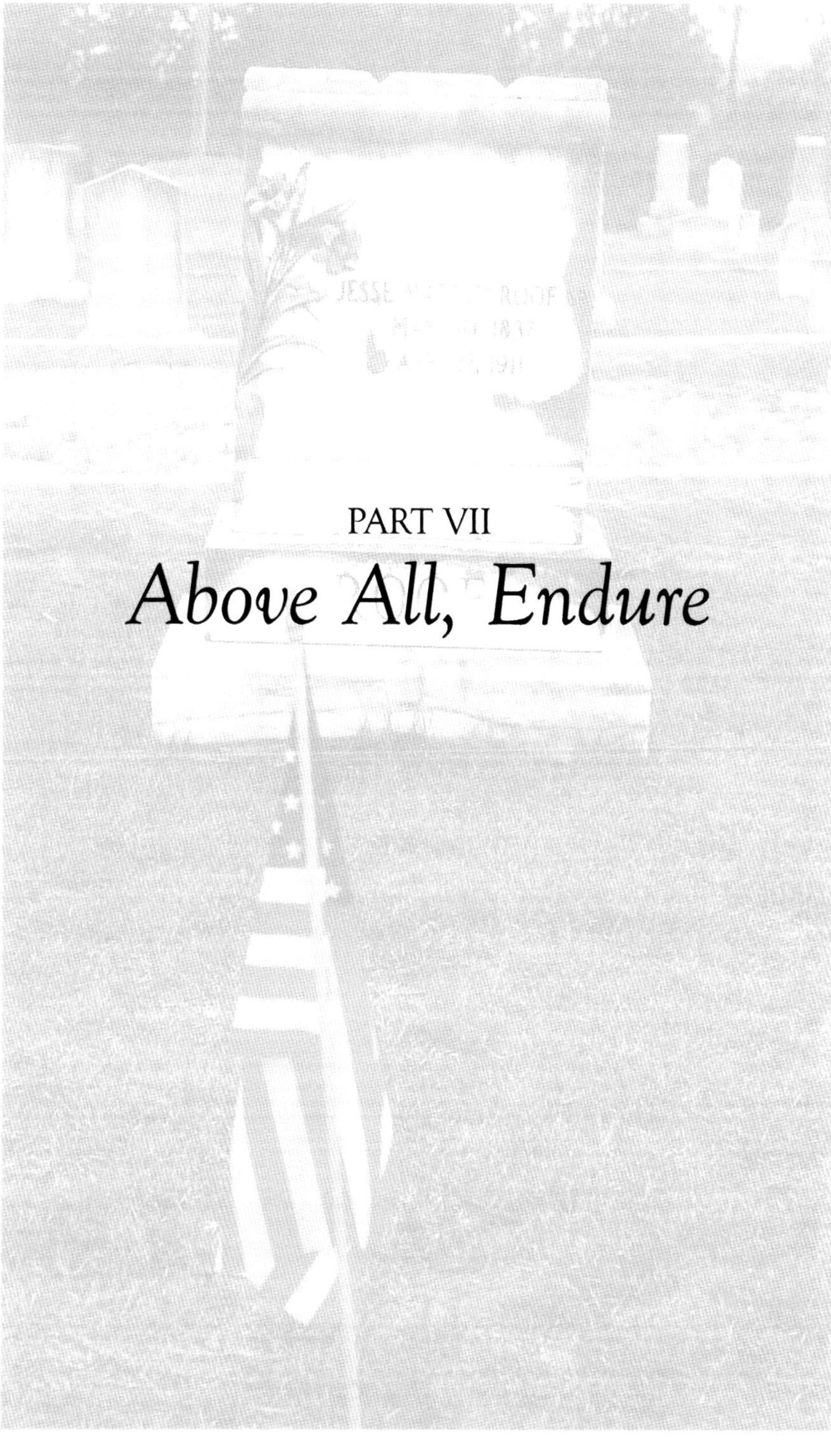

The Curly Headed Rebel

Francis Rydona Roof Wingard (February 4, 1860–August 3, 1938) was five years old when Sherman's army moved through Lexington County. Francis was the elder daughter of Jesse Marion Roof and Mary Ann "Tarsy" Shealy Roof and granddaughter of Daniel David and Amanda Sox Ruff. The family home was in White Rock at the current site of the Lowman Home.

Jesse Marion was away at war and Francis was staying in the care of relatives at the family's Lexington home near the Sycamores (which is now owned by Rex and Anneleis Bumgarner, who graciously provided the following letter). Francis wrote:

> *Why I hate war!*
> *…I saw men building a fire at one corner of the* [gin] *house. I ran with a stick and knocked out the fire. They told me they would not burn my gin house. I fought it out three times and they called me a curly white-headed rebel. He then took me by the hand and led me away, back to the house, but the gin house was covered with fire and all the barns were burning.*

This letter verifies family accounts of the day's horrors. It is told that Yankee soldiers sent flaming arrows onto the roof of the dwelling house and that, too, would have burned, except for the following:

> *…a boy was dragging wet blankets over the top of the dwelling house. My Delcie was dipping the blankets in water and throwing them up to him.*

The house was saved, but the soldiers rummaged all day until nothing was left. The family had nothing to eat, and the milk cow lay dead in the barn lot.

> *We got so hungry we could hardly walk. I went with the little Negroes and some other folks and picked up grains of corn, and grandmother boiled them in lye and made lye hominy, but I could not eat it, but that was all we had.*

This grain was probably collected from animal droppings.

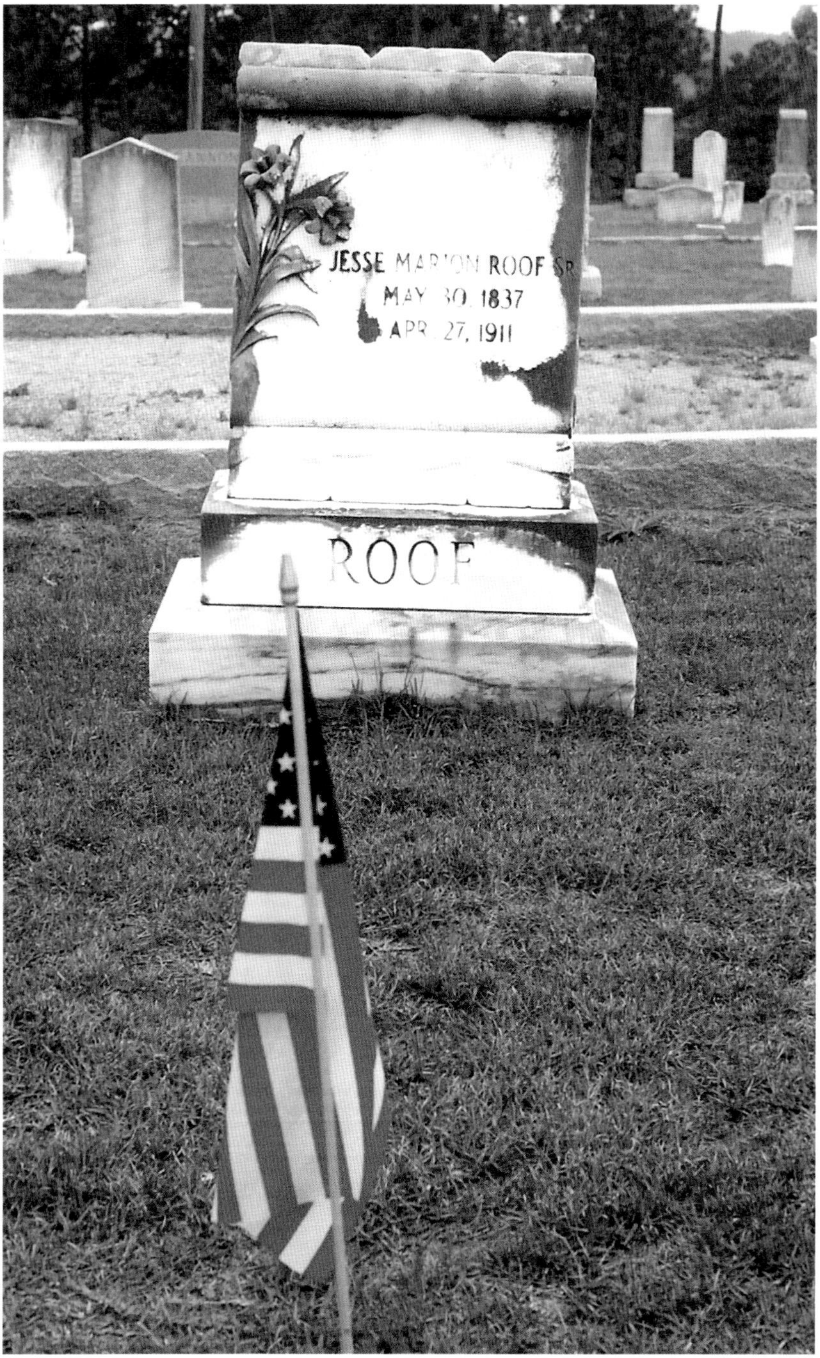

Jesse Marion Roof is buried at St. David's Lutheran Church, near the family's old homestead.

Francis's Uncle Joe came to their assistance and reunited the children with their mother, who was in White Rock. He managed to put together a buggy from parts and found an old horse the army had left behind.

> *We set off to see what had become of mother, we could hardly wait. The old horse was so slow and the road so bad we traveled all day to get to Lexington. We had to ford the river at Dreher's ford* [Lake Murray dam]. *When we arrived home you can imagine the happy meeting when my brother and I saw mother was alive as we were. We were afraid she was dead.*

Jesse Marion and Tarsy Shealy Roof had seven children, five of whom were born after the war ended.

Seventh Son of a Seventh Son

The seventh son of a seventh son, according to tradition, has special abilities. He can see into the hearts of men, know their innermost thoughts and show the way to a healing peace. Jesse Marion Roof was such a man. Jesse Marion Roof, this special child, was the son of Daniel David and Nancy Amanda Caroline Sox Roof. He was born on May 30, 1837, on the family's plantation on Platt Springs Road.

As a child, he was a first-generation Sunday schooler at St. David's Lutheran Church. In January 1859, Jesse Marion married Tarsy Shealy of White Rock. They cleared land and built a home in Lexington County. It wasn't too long before their farm began to prosper. But this pleasant life was not to last. War was brewing. At the outbreak of the Civil War, Jesse Marion volunteered and was sent to Charleston. Jesse Marion served as captain of a ship carrying supplies to Fort Sumter. He also transported dead and wounded to Charleston.

While her husband was away at war, Tarsy managed the family farm, and by that time they had three small children, Francis, Rhydona and Jesse Davis. When the Yankees came through Lexington in 1865, they attempted to burn down the Roof house, killed the milk cow and carried away the family's food supply. That left the children with nothing to eat. But God was looking out for the family of the seventh son of a seventh son, and an old spotted milk cow found its way to the Roof farm. From that day on, until the year 1940, the Roof family always kept a spotted milk cow on the place for good luck.

In 1862, Lincoln freed the slaves of the Confederacy, but Jesse Marion Roof's slaves refused to leave the Roof family. They and their descendants stayed on with the Roof family until 1923, when the last of their descendants died. These loyal people were Della and Jim Kelch and Jim Valentine.

These slave descendants held a high status on the Roof farm and were placed in charge of the most important responsibilities. They considered other farmworkers transients.

Jesse and Tarsy had five more children: Sallie, Swinton, Kate, Ida and David Werts. Jesse Marion died in April 1911. Tarsy died in March 1893. They are buried at St. David's Church near their home.

The Roberts Homestead

John Adam Roberts (1794–1882) was the son of Solomon and Mary Harmon Roberts. John Adam was married to Tembora "Tempy" Rauch (1802–1880), daughter of Jacob and Elizabeth Kyzer Rauch.

John Adam and Tempy Roberts built their home on land given to them by Tempy's father sometime after their marriage by Godfrey Dreher in 1824. Tempy's father also deeded land for a church to Providence Church elders in 1869.

John Adam served as a private in the War of 1812 in Juhan's Battalion, South Carolina Militia. John Adam and Tempy raised nine children. They were: Mary Louannie, Sarah Elizabeth, John Solomon, Jacob, Eliza Louise Priscilla, Henry Pickens, Julia C., Lucy M. and George Elias. All of the boys served the Confederacy during the Civil War, and the girls were known for their beautiful quilts.

During Sherman's march through Lexington County, part of his battalion encamped on Rauch lands in the vicinity of the Providence parsonage. The Yankee soldiers took sport in burning local homesteads and made a failed attempt at burning the Robertses' homestead. Thanks to Tempy, they had to be satisfied with ruining everything in the home with the family's supply of cane syrup. That was bad enough, but the home was spared. The soldiers also carried off as many of the beautifully made quilts as they could under their saddles.

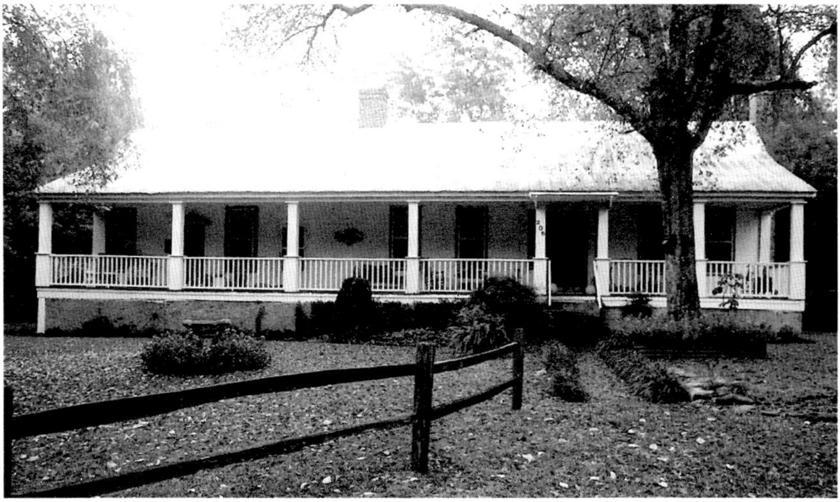

The Robertses' homestead in the Providence Church community.

In recent years, the home has been owned by the late writer-historian Lee Gandy and most recently is the residence of Heidi S. Black and her family. Heidi has operated a home-based business there, Bringing you Baskets.

Sparkin' in the Dutch Fork

Writers like to paint our imaginations with magnolias and violins when describing courtship in the antebellum South, but Dutch Fork sparkin' rituals were more likely set among the hymnbooks and fiddles in the pinetops. Aunt Katie Monts lived in the Dutch Fork all of her one hundred years, and through her stories we learn much about Dutch Fork courtship.

Sunday was the time of gathering for the young folks. Church and singing school always provided an opportunity for a young man to spark a young lady. This he did by first asking to ride along with her on her way home from church. It might be weeks before he summoned enough courage to sit a spell with her in the parlor.

Timber cutting also offered a time to socialize. Everyone in the community came to help clear land. Women came to cook, and men chopped down the timber. At dusk, as the older folks returned home, the young folks gathered around the clearing for an evening of square dancing to "Twistification," "Blackberry Pie" and sometimes the Virginian Reel.

Dutch Forkers often came to the old Summer's place in election years to eat barbecue, hear candidates' speeches and dance to Dave Hipp's fiddling as Nick Counts called the moves. No one suspected these idyllic times were nearing an end.

It is told that cannons could be heard all the way to St. Paul's Church as Fort Sumter was being fired upon. Many of the Dutch Fork's young men were in Charleston that day of the bombardment, which began at 4:30 a.m. of one day and lasted through the morning of the next. Walter and Mike Monts, George and W.C. Shealy, Hamilton and Walter Koon and Wilson Long were but a few who enlisted in the First Regiment, Kershaw's Brigade. The boys drilled at the muster field at Little Mountain before shipping out to Lightwood Knot Springs at Columbia, and finally on to Hardeeville, where they became regular soldiers.

Mothers, sisters and sweethearts came to the train station to see the soldiers off, bringing gifts of remembrance. Aunt Katie wrote a farewell message to her sweetheart, Mike Monts, in his autograph album: "A thousand tongues would fail to tell; How I esteem soldiers and how well. And may, Oh may, fair freedom glow, 'Til Heaven's last thunder shall shake this world below."

With a farewell kiss and promise to write, the train pulled out of the station at Pomaria.

War Brides of a Different Era

After Mike Monts came home in 1865, he and Katie Feagle planned to wed. Mike returned home in July after four long years at Antietam, the Wilderness, Savage Station, Petersburg, Seven Pines, Deep Bottom, Manassas and Gettysburg.

Near the end of the war, Mike was captured at Harpers Ferry and spent the winter at Camp Chase, Ohio, and Point Lookout, Maryland. He was released in July 1865 and sailed home to Charleston. He and three others walked from Charleston to Columbia, feeding themselves by begging for food. From Columbia, Mike then managed to catch a wagon ride to within a mile of home in the Dutch Fork.

It wasn't an easy adjustment for him at first. Not being used to living in a house, Mike slept on the porch. In time, he asked Katie Feagle to marry him. Marriage seemed to be on the minds of many of the young folks of the community.

Cotton was a prime crop of the Dutch Fork farmer. That fall, when the crop came in, farmers prepared to take their cotton to the Augusta market. Nearly everyone who could make the trip went along on the two-and-a-half-day journey, camping at night in their wagons and tents.

Augusta was a pleasant town with wide, tree-lined streets where shoes, stockings, calico, ribbons and supplies could be purchased. On this trip, the girls shopped for lace and yards of white silk for their wedding gowns. Lizzie Counts, Ellen Kempson and Katie Feagle shared the cost of a fine bobbinet veil, which each used at her wedding.

Mike and Katie were married on November 23, 1865, at the Feagle home. More than a hundred guests came—all the relatives on both sides of the family and all of their neighbors. No one was left out.

After the ceremony, performed by the Reverend Blackwelder, a huge dinner was served outdoors on long banquet tables. Reverend Blackwelder and the wedding party sat at the foot of the table with other guests filling in the rest. Everyone was served a wedding feast of roast pork, hash, rice, cabbage, coleslaw, beets, rice pudding, pound cake and coffee.

After dinner, it was common practice to have a cakewalk. The bride and groom led a procession of other couples around the house while passing a stick until the blast of a shotgun sounded. The couple holding the stick when the gun went off got the cake, but good manners demanded that they cut the cake and share it with the rest of the wedding guests. With that, the young folks of the Dutch Fork set about the task of rebuilding homesteads and families that had been delayed by long years of separation and war.

Henry Summer's Ordeal

Pioneer founder of the Dutch Fork German settlements John Adam Summer had many noteworthy descendants. One of these was his great-grandson, Henry Summer, born April 11, 1809, who practiced law in Lexington, Newberry and Alabama. Henry was married to Frances Mayer, sister of O.B.

Mayer Sr. They had two children: John and Kate. Henry was elected to the South Carolina House of Representatives in 1846 and 1848, representing Lexington, Newberry, Edgefield and Abbeville Districts as a member of the Cooperative Party. Henry Summer also served as secretary of the Newberry College board of trustees for many years.

On Saturday, February 19, 1865, Henry Summer faced one of his most challenging moments. As Sherman's army marched on Columbia, Summer moved his family to the family farm, which was located on the western bank of the Broad River between Columbia and Alston. Frances Summer wrote of the days' events:

> *While looking with much fear on all this, we were greatly alarmed at seeing a body of ferocious looking men charging up the Lexington Road that crossed the Prosperity Road in front of our house. They surrounded and entered the house, and the work of plunder began. We realized that we were helpless, with no friend near us; we were at the mercy of thousands of lawless men under no restraint. My husband had hoped that his age and feeble health would shield him from abuse and violence, but the events of the day proved his mistake.*
>
> *…As soon as I learned that Kilpatrick was at the front steps, he did not enter the house, but his staff and others crowded into my room where my children and I were. I made my way unaided to him, and begged unsuccessfully for protection.*
>
> *After Kilpatrick left and the sun went down, the horrors of the night began. Three or four of the savages forced him to go with them to the barn, and while they were putting a rope around his neck, demanded his gold and silver. They then made him stand on a sill, and again demanded gold. They threw the rope over a peg high up the wall, and my husband believing death was very near, closed his eyes and offered an audible prayer for himself and those who were about to murder him. His prayer saved him and he was told to come down.*

The next day, Sunday, the Summers' home was torched and the family made its way to the home of Henry's brother, William, four miles away. Eventually, the Summer family moved to Newberry, where Henry died on January 3, 1869.

Henry Summer was the son of Captain John Summer of Pomaria. His mother was the daughter of William Frederick Houseal of Lexington District, and his paternal great-grandfather was John Adam Summer, founder of the German settlement of Little Mountain in the Dutch Fork of South Carolina. His grandfather, Nicholas Summer, was at Granby during the Revolutionary War. Henry had two brothers, Adam and William Summer.

Manuel Simeon Corley

(February 10, 1823–November 20, 1902)

> *Kind words never die. The kind words and offered deeds of Comrade Corley and his father-in-law are just as fresh in memory as it was fifty-seven years ago, when it was offered. Such a generous offer like that from a friend and life-long patron was never heard of by this humble scribe, especially to a hungry, dirty, rebel prisoner, when the chances seemed that the debt could never be paid.*
>
> *—P.I. Rawl, Company K, Twentieth South Carolina Volunteers, CSA*

Simeon Corley was a man of rare conviction in a time sharpened by the clash of unresolved issues arising out of revolution. There is a temptation to call these issues political, but in truth they are far more encompassing. They are issues of the human spirit expressing its freedom—a desire for liberty. With persistence and determination, Simeon Corley pursued a quest for truth, placing virtue above safety or comfort.

Simeon Corley was the grandson of two of Lexington District's most prominent citizens, American Patriot Laurance Corley and the Reverend Yost Metz, a founder of the Lutheran Church in Lexington District. Simeon was married to Martha A. Richardson (b. April 12, 1828, d. June 14, 1908) of Tonbridge, Vermont. His father-in-law was his benefactor and supporter during his lifetime. By trade, he was a tailor; by declaration, he was an abolitionist and Unionist. Simeon Corley's family was the wellspring of his beliefs and fortitude. If indeed piety fired Simeon Corley's love of liberty, his family was his buttress. The spiritual niche his forebears carved from the colonial wilderness, Simeon sought to carve from a political wilderness.

Simeon Corley was educated at the Lexington Academy, which he attended for four years. He grew up in a community where German was frequently spoken in homes, including his own. His eloquence and command of English tells us much of the quality of education he received. From 1855 to 1856, he was editor of the *South Carolina Temperance Standard*, and there is little doubt about his political leanings or his activism and commitment to his cause. In

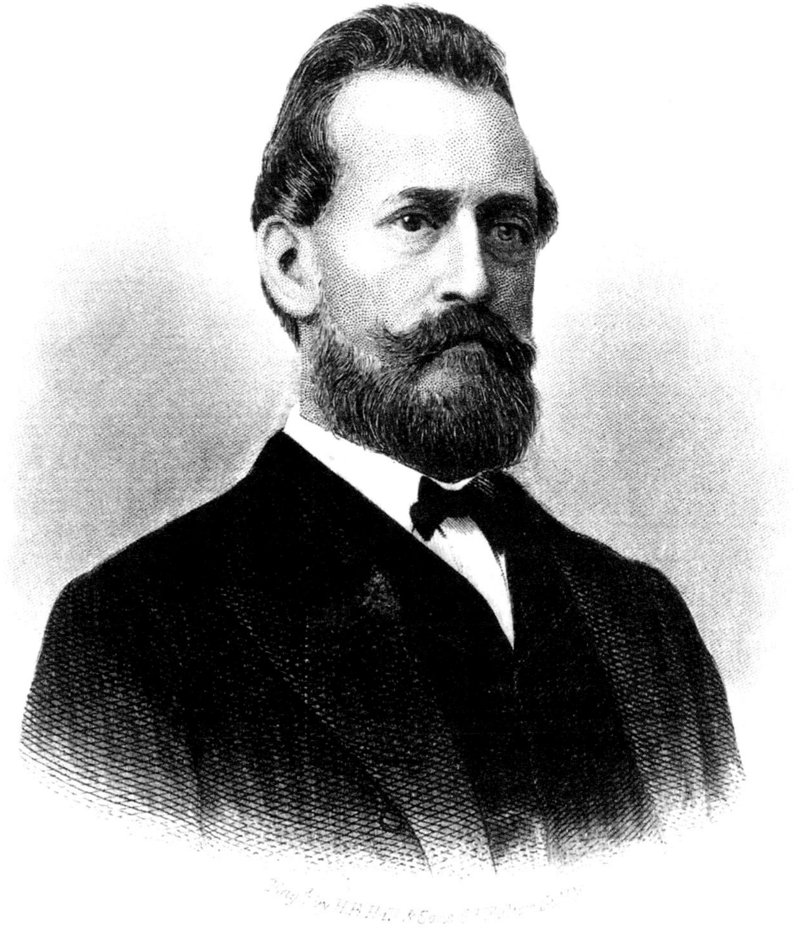

The Honorable Simeon Corley of Lexington served in Congress as a Republican in 1868.

1852, the twenty-eight-year-old Simeon was nearly expelled from the state for his opposition to South Carolina's growing secessionist sentiment. In 1865, as Columbia lay in ruins in the aftermath of Sherman's march through the Carolinas, Simeon Corley's words sprang up from the smoldering ashes like a phoenix.

The following letter by S. (Simeon) Corley was published in the *Columbia Banner* in September 1851:

Are We Free

This question has often suggested itself to my mind within the past six months. I fear we are not quite as free as free men ought to be, and that we are bound by despotism as fateful to civil and religious liberty as any other that has preceded it. Are these fears groundless? Look at the facts:

In the year 1850 a part of the citizens of Lexington District formed what they saw fit to so term a Southern Rights Association. The great object of the Association was to protect the rights and honor of the state.

With such a definition of its object, any patriot might have signed the constitution of said Association, and many doubtless did, and were not a whit more bound after doing so, to any particular measure of offense or defense than they were before. Every member was as free to decide what the rights and honor of the state were, as well as the best means to secure both, as he was before he became a member. Whenever a citizen of another nation takes the oath of allegiance to the State and the United States, it will readily be inferred by all men of common sense, that it is in sum and substance to protect and defend the rights and honor of the same. We who are native-born Carolineans and citizens of the United States by birth are bound by birth to that oath and dare not at the peril of our all, set aside that obligation. How lame then, if even the State were in danger, to get up an association without any specified object, with a constitution which asks, will you sign this? Viz: "defend the rights and honor of the State?" When, at the same time, we are sworn to do so, independent of any association. A nice opinion, really, of the knowledge, virtue, and patriotism of the people!

But the scheme, shabby as it is, was really the best that demagogues could manufacture for their own purposes. While it was the asserted principle of the Association to defend the rights and honor of the State, "the knowing ones" laid it down among themselves what was to constitute the platform of Southern orthodoxy. By this double-dealing, they managed to get a number of signatures that they could not have obtained in the plain avowal of what has transpired within the society, which plainly shows that their object is to destroy and not to defend rights.

A Mr. Wise living near Sandy Run was reported to the Association by some "patriotic" citizen and consequently a member of that honorable body, as unsound in some of his views of patriotism, rights, and honor square with the secret standards said Association. Mr. Wise failing to do so, a bill of excommunication and banishment was issued by this modern Southern Rights Inquisition. Whether Mr. Wise lopped off the excrescencies of his judgment and made it conform more nearly with their want of it, I am unable to say;

however, at a subsequent meeting of these high, holy, and infallible sovereign, the sentence of Mr. Wise was generously set aside and that gentleman allowed the privilege of remaining at home, at least, for a season. It has been stated since that time, which I hope is not true, that Mr. Wise had a tract of land which he refused to sell and others wanted it badly, but were unable to get as long as Mr. Wise was allowed to remain on it (or be banished). This is Southern Rights with a vengeance! If there is an American whose blood does not boil at the thought of such an outrage upon the freedom of opinion and speech of an honest and upright fellow citizen, he has no patriotism that a free man could envy. No wonder these giant pygmies wish to dissolve the Union, since freedom of speech and press are guaranteed by that sacred compact.

At a meeting since that trial of Mr. Wise, a Mr. Spires has been arraigned for favoring the Union. Mr. Spires says: "That in speaking of the probable disruption of the Union, at his own house, with several of his neighbors, he jokingly said he would join the North." Forthwith, some of those same friends came with their dreadful tale to the Inquisition, and said Mr. Spires was arraigned for trial. But after making a statement in his own defense and the witness against him not appearing, he was discharged.

Thus, has the Southern Rights Association again set at defiance the law of nations, the rights of man, and the provisions of the Constitution of the United States.

I am opposed to such despotism and from the assailing of Mr. Wise, I have regarded them as they are, a band of outlaws, instead of protectors of Southern or any other kind of just rights. At the meeting in March, last, my name was reported to their Secret Society Committee, as a renegade to Southern Rights. A resolution was passed that S. Corley must appear and answer to the charge at the next meeting in July. July came, but the gentleman who had the nice business of summoning me failed to discharge his important and highly patriotic part, and the case was consequently laid over for the meeting in October next. About the first of the present year, on hearing my opinions pretty freely, one nice young man made his appearance at my shop door on Saturday night, and closed his week's labor rascaling by blackening my sign. He thus transformed what was mine into his own, and it is now a pretty good indication of his business, and about as fully and blackly daubed as his character.

I have good reason to believe that this same gentleman was the identical rascal that robbed our Temperance Society of the bust of O'Neall by burglarously entering the Court House at night and after painting it by different process hung it in the street.

I believe this same gentleman has been the great champion of Southern Rights, in bringing my name before the Safety Committee of the Inquisition. However, be that as it may, I am to be tried: and for what? A difference of opinion! By whom? A band of outlaws!

Well, my friends, if you are not a nice set of defenders of right, I would like to see some of the sort! Do you know that the laws of my country protect me in the freedom of opinion and speech? Do you know that your measures are revolutionary and oppressive to the great portion, if not all of the people? Do you know that a man can fight for the Union and his State as easily as to fight for his State alone?

Suppose you pass your bill of banishment, who is to execute it? What security would your deputies have for their lives, in the plain and open violation of the law, in such a crusade upon the rights of an offending citizen? Were he to defend himself with all the means of self-preservation, and the assailant were to perish in the conflict, or he himself slain in defense of his inalienable rights, where would the guilt lie? Are you prepared for such an issue? Be assured that sooner or later, your blind madness and folly, if persisted in, will bring forth some such fruit, as proof of the hotbed upon which it flourished.

The most of you gentlemen have known me from my cradle. I am no stranger among you. You have also known my opinions: I have never kept them back. What you do not know, you can have at any time. If they are of sufficient importance to demand trial for treason, do carry it to the proper tribunal.

Some of you are members of the same church to which I belong, and profess to know the same saving power of the doctrine of Jesus Christ. Do give yourselves the trouble, for your own sakes, to examine how far your conduct accords with His spirit. Some of you are Temperance men! Do try to exercise the principle a little more in matters pertaining to the Inquisition…

I am still unwilling to aid you in pulling down the pillars upon which the glorious American Union rests; unwilling to hasten a conflict that will end in your utter destruction, and will leave you a by-word of reproach (if not utterly forgotten) to all generations; unwilling to help you to lay your homes in smoldering ruins—to see your fields deluged with the blood of your children—to leave your wives and daughters to the brutal outrage of an infuriated Negro population.

I would rather meet your scorn and contempt than fail to discharge my duty to my country and my God. My cause is the cause of truth, and with a firm reliance upon its author, I trust I am ready at all times to defend the rights and honor of the State and the United States; and if need be to meet the cannon's mouth or the tortures of your Inquisition in defense of civil and religious liberty.

Simeon Corley voluntarily served in the Confederate army as a private. He was captured by Union soldiers at Petersburg, Virginia, on April 2, 1865, in the last days of the war and was taken as a prisoner to the U.S. Prison Camp at Point Lookout, Maryland.

Simeon Corley went on to serve as special agent of the treasury in 1869, Lexington County treasurer in 1874 and commissioner of agricultural statistics of South Carolina in 1879. He served six years as treasurer of the South Carolina Lutheran Synod and was a lifelong member of St. Stephen's Lutheran Church. He died November 20, 1902, at the age of seventy. Simeon and his wife Martha are both buried at St. Stephen's Church, Lexington.

Camp Sorghum

In the waning months of the Civil War, Northern prisoners of war were sent to the Carolinas as the Confederate government attempted to reduce populations of some of the more infamous prison camps such as Andersonville.

One such camp was Camp Sorghum, located in Columbia near the Saluda River. There were said to have been 1,370 prisoners in the camp. Conditions at Camp Sorghum have been recorded in the personal journals of men held captive in this camp. These journals were later published as books, such as *Prisoners of War and Military Prisons* by Asa B. Isam and *The Army Experiences of Captain James Donaghy*, that go into great detail about their experiences at Camp Sorghum. The following is the account of Captain James Donaghy.

On the afternoon of October 6, 1864, the prison train arrived in Columbia.

In the midst of a cold, pouring rain we moved into an open lot in the outskirts of the city where the night was passed lying upon the ground without shelter. The next day we marched three miles south of the city, and for permanent quarters, turned into an open field having upon it a thin growth of stubby pines. The weather was rainy and cold; we were in a sorry plight for clothing

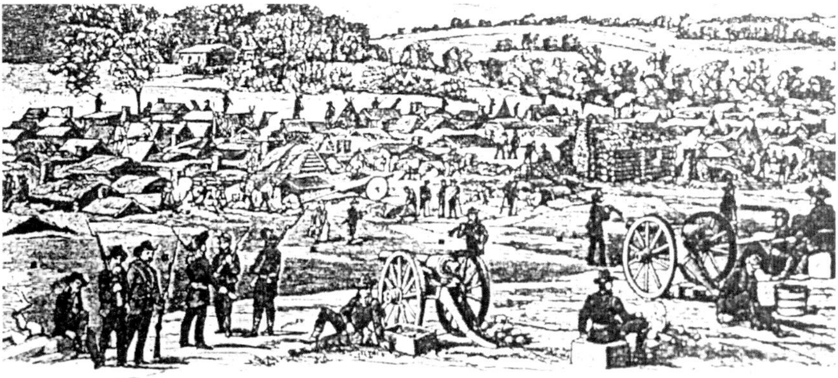

A sketch of Camp Sorghum, West Columbia.

and shoes, the majority having but shreds for clothing and many being shoeless. On the 9th of October a distribution of clothing was sent by the United States Sanitary Commission.

The only ration issued was corn meal, salt, and sorghum molasses. From this last named article the place was dubbed Camp Sorghum. The sorghum was a good article, but with corn meal it gave rise to an intense and acid dyspepsia and diarrhea, so that we were compelled to throw it away.

Any one who has not suffered from prolonged meat deprivation can imagine the cravings which tormented us. Anything having the appearance of meat would have been greedily devoured and no questions asked. An old razorback boar as tough, lean and unsavory as an aged billy goat, upon straggling into camp, was set upon and dispatched with clubs. The famished prisoners piled upon each other in the struggle to get a piece of the flesh and hacked it up into little pieces with knives.

Escape Was Common

At Columbia escapes were made by the wholesale, one hundred at a time. It was the custom to let a hundred in one party, under parole, go out into the woods after firewood. While this squad was out another hundred would form in line at the dead line awaiting their turn. These would often be allowed to pass out before the other returned. Then a hundred, who had been given no parole, would form in line, and confusing the guard in regard to the squads that had passed in and out, they would also be allowed to move out. When they reached the woods, they scattered themselves in depressions which they had covered over with brush and when night came they struck out for freedom.

Many prisoners were so weak and poorly shod they had no chance of escape when they did get it. Nevertheless, they improved every opportunity to obtain a breath of free air, even though it might be for but an hour and at great personal hazard.

Gold in Camp Sorghum

Among the prisoners were men who had been California gold miners and they discovered indications of gold in the bed of the stream and set to work washing out some of the sand. Their manner of working to fill a tin pan with the sand and shake it about in the running water, allowing the sand that would rise to pass over the rim of the pan and away. The small particles of gold that were in the sand would settle to the bottom of the pan till at last all the sand would be washed away and a few tiny specks of the precious metal would remain. The old miners estimated that with proper facilities for working a man could earn Two Dollars a day in the stream.

Many years after the war ended, several of the camp's former prisoners revisited the site, remembering their experiences there.

PART VIII

Overcoming and Prosperity

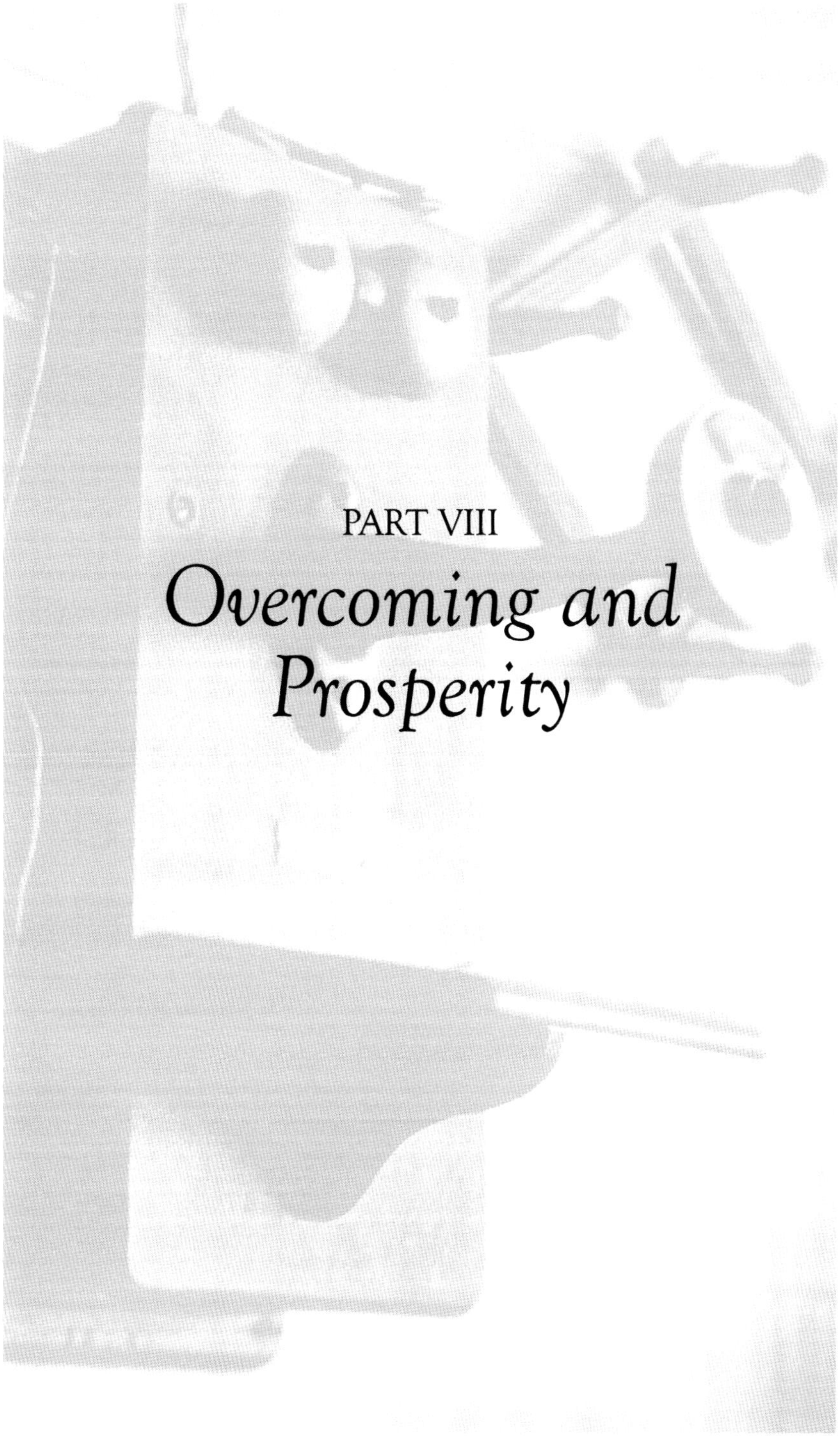

The Comet of 1843

The comet of 1843 appeared in the Dutch Fork in early January of that year, but it wasn't the first comet sighting. The following text is taken from Orlando B. Mayer's tale, "The Cob-Pipe."

The comet of 1843 was appropriately named for Mark Moyer, the fellow who first "received the image of the phenomenon upon his retina" on a cold January night while hunting 'possum in the church-wood of St. John's, Pomaria. Moyer related this account of the event to his companions the following day:

> *Fellers, I was 'possum hunting last night in de church-woods down yonder, and when I got to the graveyard where I could see all around in the firmament and could look over tree tops, I suddenly seed de frightfulest white streak in de sky wat was ever hearn tell of. I 'clare boys, de water started in my eyes fast, and jest den I disciver'd dat de ting was alive; for it commenced to move itself like a serpunt, and it darted out o' its head a forky tongue what reach'd away up in de firmament to Job's Coffin, and a string out o' its tail as tetch'd de top of a high pine tree. I tell you, I couldn't stand it: I had to drap my 'possum and make tracks.*
>
> *…I concluded I would come by de church, as dare was preachin' here today, and tell de people wat I seed. For my part, I believe de Day of Judgmint will come along here by sunset today.*

The Great Earthquake of 1886

The date was August 31, 1886. The time 9:51 p.m. The killer quake had two epicenters, both in the Charleston and Summerville area. Tremors from this quake were felt as far away as Wisconsin, nearly a thousand miles distance. Ninety-two people in South Carolina died.

Throughout South Carolina, tremors continued into the night. Most folks of the Dutch Fork and Lexington had gone to bed for the night. As the earth trembled, family members grabbed chairs and mattresses and went into the yard for safety. In the distance, they felt the earth rumble as shock after shock rolled through the red lands and sandy hills.

Katie Monts recalled the night:

> *We watched our house rock, heard the widows rattle, and the bowls and pitchers in the bedrooms tossing around. Everything seemed queer. The cows all over the neighborhood were lowing, the roosters crowed in distress, seeming to sense something unusual. Dogs barked. I remember there were a number of petunias in our front yard in full bloom. They shook so pitifully, not as though the wind were blowing, but as if they had a chill.*

Lexington's Trial of the Century

Lexington County is known for its tough, conservative prosecutors. In 1903, a notorious murder trial proved to be as vexing as the O.J. Simpson trial of the 1990s. The case was *South Carolina v. James H. Tillman*. Tillman, nephew of "Pitchfork Ben" Tillman, had murdered the publisher and editor of the *State* newspaper, N.G. Gonzales, near the state capital on January 15, 1903.

Tillman, lieutenant governor and gubernatorial candidate, pled self-defense in the shooting of the unarmed Gonzales. Witnesses were impeached by being labeled Republican. The defense openly declared the right of revenge for libelous public name-calling. In the end, a Lexington jury found Tillman innocent of the charges.

The murder occurred in 1903, but the anger that caused it began many years before. This assassination was about two rival families of dynastic proportions—the Gonzales and the Tillman families.

General Ambrosio Gonzales came to South Carolina in 1848 as a political refuge from Havana, Cuba, after the unsuccessful Cuban revolt against Spain. Gonzales married a South Carolinian, Harriet Rutledge Elliott of Beaufort.

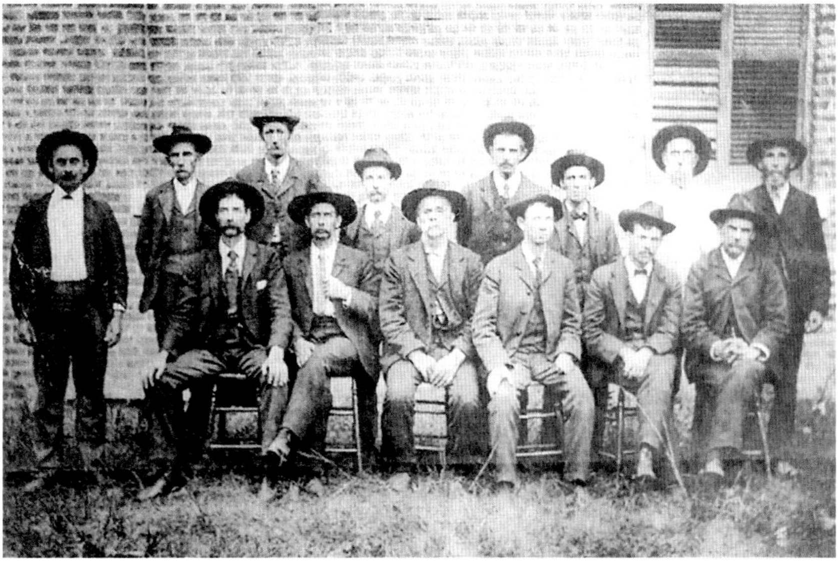

The Tillman versus Gonzales jury at Lexington Court in 1903. This jury found James Tillman not guilty of murdering N.G. Gonzales.

Harriet was a descendant of Henry Woodward, William Rhett and at least three South Carolina governors.

Harriet and Ambrosio had four sons and three daughters. Three of these sons—Ambrose, Narsisco Gener "N.G." and William Elliott—distinguished themselves in South Carolina's history. The family lived a life of wealth and luxury on the family's Beaufort plantation.

General Gonzales served the Confederacy under General Beauregard. After the Confederate war, the family retreated to Cuba, where Harriet died. Upon their return to South Carolina, they found their plantation stripped and their wealth gone.

The boys were educated at Grahamville and served apprenticeships. Ambrose became a traveling representative for the *Charleston News and Courier* in 1885, and in 1889 he came to Columbia to serve as secretary of the Department of Agriculture. In 1891, he helped N.G. organize the *State* newspaper.

N.G. was educated at a Spanish-speaking school in Matanzan and at Grahamville. While still at Grahamville, he began writing for the *Charleston News and Courier*. In 1890, when Ben Tillman was elected governor, N.G. resigned his post at the *News and Courier* and established the *State* newspaper on February 18, 1891, with a vow to expose unworthy people and unsound politics.

The Murder

The date was January 15, 1903. N. G. Gonzales had spent most of the morning at the statehouse. The 1903 session was just beginning, and a new governor was to be inaugurated in a matter of days. N.G.'s mission on this day was to draw an attack from an old opponent—to "rub salt into the wounds his shaft had opened." After leaving the statehouse, he went to the *State* newspaper office. At almost 2:00 p.m., he left to go home for lunch. As he crossed Main Street wearing his heavy overcoat with his hands tucked deeply into the pockets, he met a group of men coming from the capital. One of these men was Lieutenant Governor James H. Tillman. As the men approached Gonzales, Tillman drew a Luger and fired it at the unarmed editor, wounding him in the abdomen. The two exchanged words. Tillman was heard to say, "I got your message." Gonzales shouted back as he turned, "Shoot again, you coward."

Tillman immediately surrendered to a policeman at the scene, while Gonzales was carried back to the newspaper office. He was taken to the old Columbia Hospital for surgery and rallied somewhat, but was unable to overcome the infection. His funeral was held on a cold and wet January day at Trinity Cathedral, with over two thousand people attending.

No account of the incident was printed in the *State*, but other papers across the state and nation carried the story, and extracts from Gonzales's editorials denouncing Tillman were printed in an effort to explain to readers what had provoked Tillman.

A long-standing personal feud had been festering between the two men. When Gonzales was editor of the *Tri-Weekly News Herald* of Winnsboro, Tillman called Gonzales a wily Spaniard of treacherous blood. Gonzales's sneering pen was quick with a rebuttal, but the most inflammatory remarks concerning lies, fraud and gambling were attributed to other papers close to Gonzales. At one point, Tillman challenged Gonzales to settle their differences on the dueling field. Gonzales declined.

In his bid for governor in 1902, Tillman ran a poor fourth in the primary, blaming Gonzales for the loss. Despite Tillman's defeat, Gonzales was unrelenting and challenged the senate to impeach Tillman because of an incident concerning a controversial debate. Then, all fell silent.

The Trial

Columbia was a hotbed of anti-Tillmanism.

In June, following the murder, Tillman's defense attorneys requested a change of venue and the trial was moved to neutral Lexington County. Lexington, however, had always delivered a large vote for Ben Tillman, and Jim Tillman's wife, Mamie, was the granddaughter of John Fox of Lexington.

There were mixed feelings about the murder throughout the state, and many expressed surprise that Gonzales had not been shot months earlier. J.C. Hemphill described the event: "If a man insists upon playing with live wires—electrocution usually results—nevertheless it is a great pity." Most editors statewide expected Tillman to be exonerated.

Tillman remained in jail until the time of the trial. From his jail cell, which had been equipped with furniture, books and flowers, he saw supporters and issued occasional statements condemning persecution by the press.

The judge and legal teams were selected. Frank B. Gary, a close Tillman ally, was to serve as judge. The Gonzales family hired Duncan Bellinger, Andrew Crawford, William Elliott Jr., Edward Lee Asbill and L. Tyrone Sturkie for the prosecution.

The solicitor was William Thurmond (Strom Thurmond's father). In the Tillman camp were George Croft, Patrick Nelson, Osmund Johnstone, W.T. Sharpe, G.T. Graham, Cole Blease, George Rembert and the Efird and Dreher law firm.

The trial began almost eight months after the crime, with the defendant pleading self-defense. A young court reporter, James F. Byrnes, was hired by the *State* to record the proceedings verbatim for publication in its court column. Lexington was full of public figures during the three-week trial. Senator Ben Tillman came for one session, even though he denounced the shooting. He later explained, "Jim Tillman is my nephew, and blood is thicker than water."

William Elliott Jr. warned that a "not guilty verdict from the jury would sanction the shooting of public-spirited editors and end freedom of the press." The defense used the inflammatory editorials to its advantage as evidence of justifiable homicide. The jury gave a not guilty verdict.

The *State* published sensational headlines—"The Crime of Lexington"—as it erected a monument to the slain Gonzales in Columbia.

South Carolina historian D.D. Wallace noted, "The Gonzales family experienced a ghastly vengeance. The ghost of the dead man pursued Jim Tillman the rest of his unhappy days." Tillman died eight years later.

Murder at the Mill

The two men lay hunkered down in the tall grass behind the fence row in the late afternoon of February 19, 1904. Their prey was at the end of the lane on the Twelve Mile Creek millpond. They were lying in wait for a neighbor, or perhaps he was their relative. No one knew for sure. This was frontier justice when that uncultivated justice was no longer tolerated. Or was it?

A woman was coming up the path to the pond where John W. Meetze was sharpening his saws. She made her way past his home, where his wife prepared their evening meal and tended to their child. She wound her way down the incline, when she spotted the two men. Catlike, she ran to tell Meetze of the trouble that awaited him.

As the two made their way up the path, two fiery shotgun blasts broke the tension—that of the assailant and its mark.

Meetze was struck by fourteen buckshot in the face and a few more in the side. The woman ran for the public road and was struck in the arm and lung. She faltered and fell, but her wounds were not bad enough to overcome her terror. She fled past the Meetze place to a home farther up the road, where a friend carried her by wagon to her employer's doctor, C.W. Barron of Brookland.

At Brookland, she sent out the alarm to Meetze's brothers, Lee and Early Meetze, who had an investigation of the crime underway by six o'clock that evening. The body lay fifteen yards from the ambush spot, and a single set of tracks led across the fence toward the Twelve Mile Creek.

Neighbors were questioned, but nothing came to light about the identity of Meetze's assailants. Sheriff Caughman spent all of the next day at the crime scene, but turned up nothing. The murder remained unsolved.

There were a few theories about the murder. Some believed Meetze's hard-drinking and turbulent disposition led to his death. Others believed the unidentified woman's relatives did him in. Still others believed that he had finally reaped his punishment for his injustice toward his family and contentiousness toward his neighbors.

Stranger still is the fact that his father was killed sixteen years earlier in the same manner at a location less than a half mile away.

Rural Free Mail Delivery

Mail delivery changed in 1863, when President Lincoln signed a bill requiring home mail delivery in cities with a population over twenty thousand. Despite the fact that 54 percent of the population lived in rural areas, it wasn't until 1896 that rural free delivery (RFD) routes were authorized.

Even then, RFD was a controversial issue in Congress. But with the supportive efforts of agricultural organizations such as the Grange, RFD eventually passed, and an experimental rural delivery was inaugurated in Charleston, Hallman and Uvilla, West Virginia. Within a year, twenty-nine states had rural routes, and by 1906 there were thirty thousand rural routes nationwide. An improved and expanded highway system followed the growth of rural mail routes. And in 1913, parcel post delivery was established, beginning the mail-order industry.

Lexington's first RFD was started on May 15, 1900. Within nine years, there were six routes. In the early 1900s, Lexington's post office was located on Main Street next to the courthouse. The following notes from RFD carrier Lonnie B. Addy tell us about these first routes.

> *Route 1 was established on May 15, 1900. Esasis L. Wingard was appointed carrier and his brother Baylis Wingard substitute. Carrier Wingard resigned in July 1908 to become a candidate for County Treasurer, and shortly after, his son Elmer F. Wingard was appointed carrier with his brother Hubbard T. Wingard substitute.*
>
> *Route Two was established about 1904. Frank B. George was appointed carrier. Thomas L. Harmon was appointed substitute. He resigned in early 1906. H.A. Meetze was then appointed, but only made a few trips before resigning. Then Thomas Wingard was appointed substitute for about eighteen months, resigning to become assistant postmaster.*
>
> *Route Three was established about February 1905. George B. Lee was the first carrier and Charles V. Bouknight was sub. A snow fell on the first day of service. Carrier walked as far as the railroad station. I, Lonnie B. Addy, saw him return to the Post Office. He resigned immediately. E. Austin Roof was then appointed and served until June 1920, resigning to become a candidate for County Sheriff.*

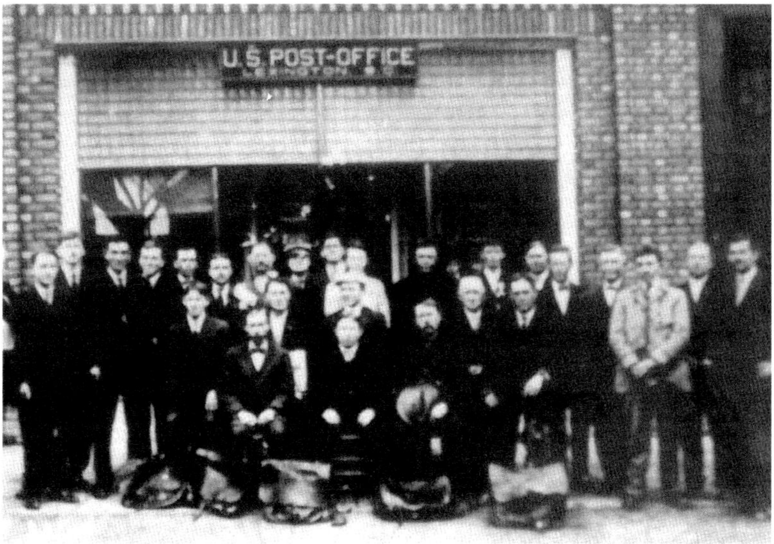

An early photo of Lexington Post Office.

Route Four was established on August 15, 1905, with Lonnie B. Addy as carrier and a Mr. Roof as substitute. This route was fourteen miles long with pay of $504 per year.

Route Five was begun on August 15, 1905, with Quincy E. Caughman as carrier and his brother W. Morgan Caughman as substitute. Caughman served until 1933, when he retired. The route was then merged into Routes Two and Three.

Route Six was established in April or May 1909, with George B. Lee as carrier and S.S. George as substitute. Lee resigned after a few months and went back to work in a cotton mill.

Mr. Bell's Marvelous Machine

Sam George was a man of remarkable insight. On a trip west in 1890, he had the good fortune to observe the telephone in operation and saw the potential it held for his hometown, Lexington. He wasn't one to sit on a good thing, so he

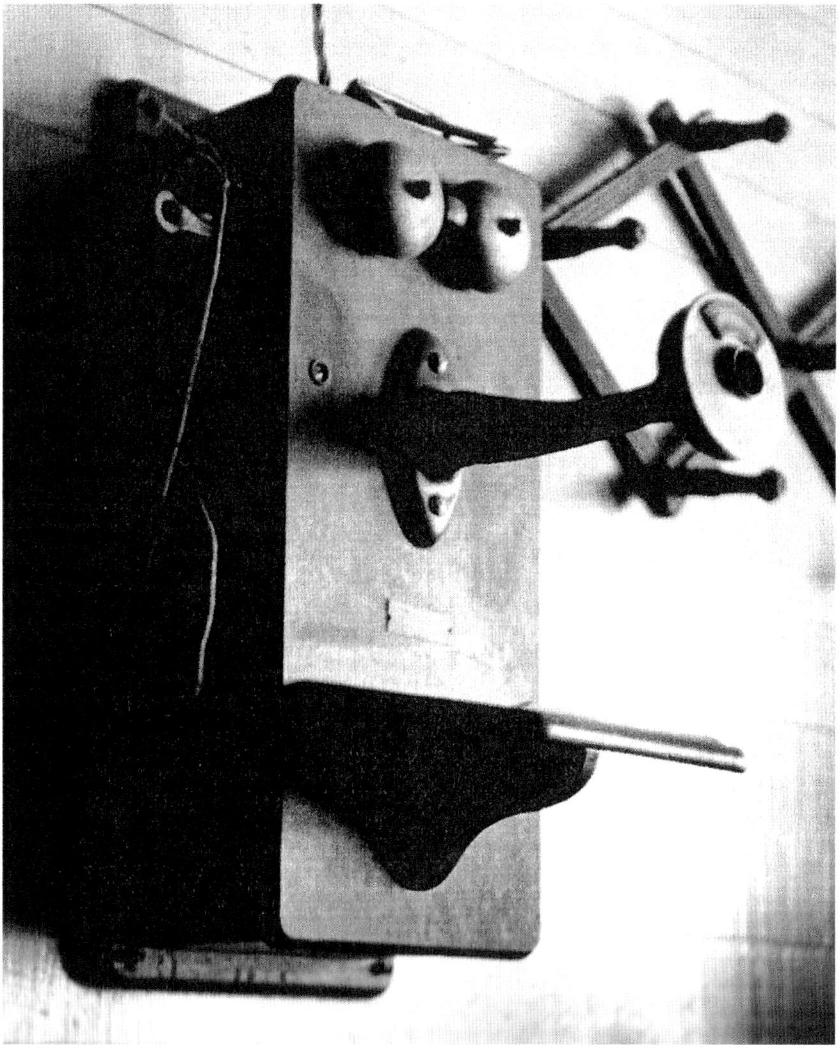

One of Lexington's first telephones.

went to work learning how to string lines and securing funds to buy equipment for his new company, Citizens Telephone Company. By 1911, there were 354 calling customers.

Citizens was a George family–owned business operating from an office above the drugstore. In 1930, the telephone company moved into an office on Main Street and had around-the-clock operators. In 1948, the company switched over to its first dial system and had grown to over five hundred customers.

About the time television came onto the market, Lexington's 1,250 callers could connect with Columbia toll-free. Citizens was growing along with the community, and there was a communications explosion. It would be another forty-two years before a digital system would connect its service under the name of Alltel Telephone Company, providing 27,000 access lines to the Lexington area.

As Sam George was setting up Citizens, James Luther Smith was installing a communication system for family members at Pond Branch. The idea caught on and soon spread throughout the community. This was the start of Pond Branch Telephone Company, which operated with a Delco system that ran on batteries charged with a water wheel.

Pond Branch began to grow, adding Gilbert, Pelion, Swansea and a toll line to Wagener. In 1929, Pond Branch had sixty subscribers. With assistance from REA loans, Pond Branch upgraded its equipment and expanded its service with a switch-dial central office. By 1969, Pond Branch's six hundred subscribers were the beneficiaries of the state's first underground telephone cable network. By 1975, all of Pond Branch's telephones were private lines that replaced the old party line system.

Pond Branch is also a family-run company. Its newest generation successfully negotiated cellular service in 1985 and today has widened its service area by 650 square miles, taking in parts of Saluda, Edgefield, Aiken, Calhoun and Orangeburg Counties.

The State Fair

South Carolina's first state fair was organized in 1869 and provided a showcase for farmers to exhibit produce, livestock and home arts. In the early 1920s, Lexington farmers Willie Edwin Corley and sons Earl Pickens and Archie Baylis Corley prepared prizewinning exhibits.

The Corleys were regular exhibitors at the state fair, and a newspaper of the day reported a story told by Willie Corley.

> *Corley is the son of Emanuel Corley who at the age of ninety died a few years ago. Emanuel Corley was a man of prodigious strength. On one occasion he is said to have picked up and carried off seven bushels of cow feed tied up*

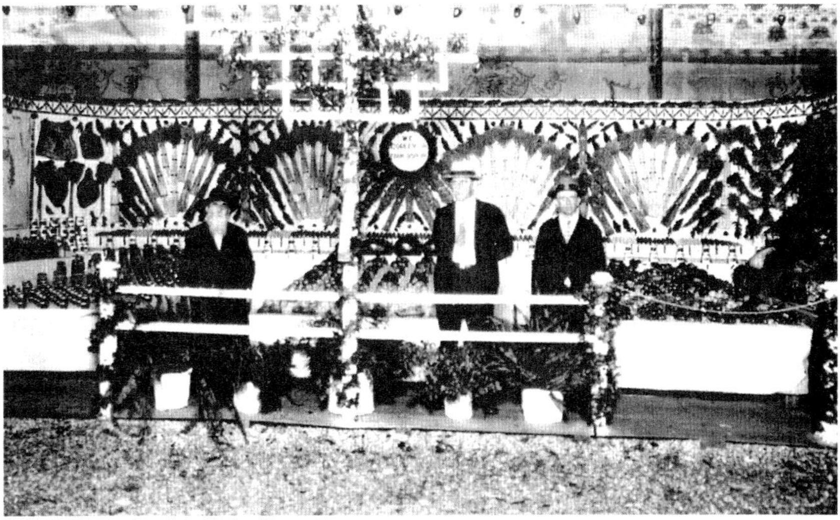

The Corley exhibit at the state fair.

> *in a sheet. Cow feed weighs sixty pounds to the bushel. His son also says his father was known to have picked up and carried off sixteen pieces of green lumber at the saw mill, each piece was sixteen feet long and ten inches wide and three-fourths of an inch thick—total weight around five hundred pounds. The average bale of cotton weighs five hundred pounds.*

In the early years, the fair was on Elmwood Avenue, which also served as a parade ground for military tournaments. Horse racing was a main attraction, with a $200 purse being offered by the trotting club. Burlesque comedians came to town, drawn by fair week audiences. They played to full houses at local hotels. Fair-going crowds were treated to a fireworks display, hot air balloons and gander pulling. Many people of the area, participant and observer alike, prided themselves on never missing a state fair.

Selected Bibliography

Batesburg-Leesville Area History. Lexington County, SC: Privately published and compiled by the Batesburg-Leesville Chamber of Commerce, 1982.

Bernham, G.D. *The History of the Lutheran Church in North and South Carolina*. N.p., 1872.

Carson, Betty, and Doris Wooley, comps. *Our Hewing Heritage with Related Families.* Vol. 2. Revised edition. Bowie, MD: Heritage Books, Inc., 1996.

Caughman, J. Ansel. *A History of the Religious Life of Cedar Grove Community and Families Influencing Its Culture*. Batesburg, SC: The Bruner Press, 1952.

Friday, Martin. *Martin Friday*. Paper from the collection of Lee Gandee.

Gandee, Lee R. *Education in Lexington County, South Carolina, Prior to the Year 1900*. Lexington, SC: n.p., 1971.

Godfrey, Harmon. *Uncle Josh: Remembrances of Old Lexington County, South Carolina*. Lexington, SC: The Lexington County Historical Society, 1940.

Green, Edwin L. *A History of Richland County, Vol. I, 1732–1805*. Columbia, SC: R.L. Bryan Company, 1932.

Hall, Lindsey G. *Things and Incidents of Long Ago*. Columbia, SC: State Printing Company, 1970.

Hallman, S.T., ed. *History of the Evangelical Lutheran Synod of South Carolina 1824–1924*. Columbia, SC: Authority of the Synod, 1924.

Hayes, Louise Frederick. *History of Macon County, Georgia*. Atlanta: Macon County Commissioners, 1933.

Hendrix, Roberta L. *The Hendrix Family of Mobile, Alabama*. Privately printed family history, 1980.

Hewatt, Alexander. *An Historical Account of the Rise and Progress of the Colonies of South Carolina and Georgia*. London: Alexander Donaldson, 1779.

History of the Synod Committee, ed. *A History of the Evangelical Lutheran Church in America*. South Carolina Synod and the Lutheran Church of America, 1971.

Lossing, Benson J. *Hours With the Living Men and Women of the Revolution: A Pilgrimage.* N.p., 1889.

Mayer, Orland B. *The Dutch Fork*. Columbia, SC: Dutch Fork Press, 1982.

———. *Fireside tales: Stories of the Old Dutch Fork*. Columbia, SC: Dutch Fork Press, 1982.

Meriwether, Robert L. *The Expansion of South Carolina, 1729–1765*. Kingsport, TN: n.p., 1940.

Milling, Chapman J. *Red Carolinians*. Columbia: University of South Carolina Press, 1969.

Neal, Rosemary Corley. *Southern Sojourners Corley—Sanford and Allied Lines*. N.p., 1991.

Oliphant, Mary Simms. *The New Sims History of South Carolina, Centennial Edition 1840–1940.* Columbia, SC: State Printing Company, 1940.

Pinckney, Roger. "Crying in the Wilderness, The Gonzales Legacy." *Sandlapper Magazine* (Spring 1999).

Quattlebaum, Paul. *The Land Called Chicora*. Spartanburg, SC: Reprint Company, 1956.

Ramsay, David. *Ramsay's History of South Carolina: From its First Settlement in 1670 to the Year 1808*. Spartanburg, SC: Reprint Company, 1959.

Salley, Alexander S. *The History of Orangeburg County, South Carolina.* Baltimore, MD: Regional Publishing Company, 1969.

Scott, Edwin J. *Random Recollections of a Long Life*. Columbia, SC: Charles A. Calvo Jr., 1884.

Sease, Elberta. *Aunt Katie 100 Years*. Columbia, SC: Dutch Fork Press, 1979.

Slocomb, Dottie Hendrix. *Hendrix Happenings*. Privately printed family history, 1997.

Wallace, David Duncan. *The History of South Carolina*. New York: American Historical Society Inc., 1934.

OTHER SOURCES

The Lexington County Public Library
South Carolina Room
5440 Augusta Road
Lexington, SC 29072

The Lexington County Museum
231 Fox Street
Lexington, SC 29072

The Cayce Historical Museum
1800 12th Street Extension
Cayce, SC 29033

The Lexington County Genealogical Association
PO Box 1142
Lexington, SC 29071

South Carolina Genealogical Society, Inc.
The Dutch Fork Chapter
PO Box 481
Chapin, SC 29036

Old Edgefield District Genealogical Society
PO Box 546
Edgefield, SC 29842

The Georgia Salzburger Society
2980 Ebenezer Road
Rincon, GA 31326

Cherokees of South Carolina
PO Box 7062
Columbia, SC 29202

South Carolina Institute of Archaeology and Anthropology
University of South Carolina
1321 Pendleton Street
Columbia, SC 29208

South Caroliniana Library
University of South Carolina
The USC Horseshoe
Columbia, SC 29208

South Carolina Department of Archives and History
PO Box 11669
Columbia, SC 29211